wills and probate
richard pooley and
jacqueline martin

For over 60 years, more than
40 million people have learnt over
750 subjects the **teach yourself**
way, with impressive results.

be where you want to be
with **teach yourself**

Rider

While this book is designed to provide accurate information with regard to its subject matter, it is not intended as a substitute for qualified legal advice and the Authors and Publisher cannot accept any claim for financial loss resulting from its use.

For UK order enquiries: please contact Bookpoint Ltd, 130 Milton Park, Abingdon, Oxon OX14 4SB. Telephone: +44 (0) 1235 827720. Fax: +44 (0) 1235 400454. Lines are open 09.00–18.00, Monday to Saturday, with a 24-hour message answering service. Details about our titles and how to order are available at www.teachyourself.co.uk

Long renowned as the authoritative source for self-guided learning – with more than 40 million copies sold worldwide – the **teach yourself** series includes over 300 titles in the fields of languages, crafts, hobbies, business, computing and education.

British Library Cataloguing in Publication Data: a catalogue record for this title is available from the British Library.

First published in UK 1999 by Hodder Education, 338 Euston Road, London, NW1 3BH.

The **teach yourself** name is a registered trade mark of Hodder Headline.

Typeset by Transet Limited, Coventry, England.
Printed in Great Britain for Hodder Education, a division of Hodder Headline, 338 Euston Road, London NW1 3BH, by Cox & Wyman Ltd, Reading, Berkshire.

Hodder Headline's policy is to use papers that are natural, renewable and recyclable products and made from wood grown in sustainable forests. The logging and manufacturing processes are expected to conform to the environmental regulations of the country of origin.

Impression number	10 9 8 7 6 5 4 3
Year	2009 2008 2007 2006 2005

contents

This book is intended for the general reader who wishes to find out about wills and/or the rules on inheritance. It is not for academics, though we also believe that it will prove useful to students who are studying law as a vocational subject. We have tried to avoid the use of technical expressions as far as possible and to keep the book free of legal jargon. However, it is sometimes necessary to understand legal expressions and so a glossary of key terms is included at the end of the book.

Using this book

Teach Yourself Wills and Probate is divided into three parts each concentrating on a different aspect of wills and probate in the United Kingdom.

The first part is about making sure your property goes where you want it to when you die. That usually depends on whether you have made a will and, if you have, whether it is valid. The opening chapter explains why you should make a will. The rest of the section takes you through what you need to consider when making a will and then goes on to the practicalities of how to make a valid will. For those who are wealthy a chapter is included on 'estate planning' indicating how it may be possible to save paying too much tax, though it must be remembered that the government can change the rules on taxation at any time.

The second part explains the rules on who inherits where there is no will. It also deals with when it is possible for someone who has not inherited to make a claim for financial provision from the estate.

The third part sets out the practicalities of dealing with the property of someone who has died. It covers both the situation where there is a will and where there is not. It explains who can apply to act as a personal representative in these situations and what their duties are.

The main focus is based on the law of England and Wales, but in each section there are separate chapters on the rules in Scotland and in Northern Ireland. The law stated is as at 30 September 2002 in relation to deaths occurring after 6 April 2002. The financial figures used are those in the Budget of April 2003.

Finally, throughout this book we have used 'he' and 'his' to include 'she' and 'hers'. The Victorians were the first to address this issue of political correctness and they resolved it by passing a law in 1889, called the Interpretation Act. That Act said, amongst other things, that words expressed in one gender in legal documents include the other gender. That rule still applies under a newer version of the Interpretation Act and we rely on that Act! On a practical level we have chosen 'he' and 'his' only because the masculine form is shorter than the feminine.

part one

making a will

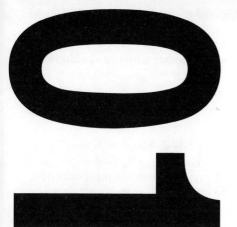

01

why make a will?

In this chapter you will learn:
- why you need to make a will
- about common misunderstandings regarding inheritance laws.

The best reason we can think of for making a will is peace of mind. In this chapter, we look at several common misunderstandings about what happens to your property when you die and we propose six good reasons why you should make a will.

If you have made a valid will and have expressed your wishes clearly, you can be confident that your property should go where you want it to.

It is a mistake to assume that the law will deal with your estate in the way you want if you do not make a will. Your wishes and the workings of the law may correspond but you must not count on this. If the thought of making a will fills you with dread, it is essential that you first find out what the law says about who will inherit your property if you do not make a will. You can then make an informed decision about the need for a will.

When we were writing this book, we came across numerous misunderstandings about what happens to a person's property upon death. Here are the most common:

- A letter written by the deceased expressing his wishes about what is to happen to his property on his death is as good as a will. FALSE

- A surviving spouse always inherits their partner's property, which they must use for the benefit of their family. FALSE

- The next of kin automatically acquires the property of the deceased and has a legal duty to distribute it fairly amongst the members of his family. FALSE

- A final request by a dying person is always enforceable. FALSE

All these are either completely wrong or partly wrong.

The following case studies, which are true stories, illustrate the misery and distress that may follow from failing to make a will.

Case study 1

Harry and his wife Joan lived in a house that they rented. Harry had built up substantial savings of about £100,000. They had three adult children, one of whom was disabled. Joan's relationship with her children was strained and unhappy. Harry had been told that he did not need to make a will because he did not own the property he lived in and that a letter would be enough to ensure that his wishes would be carried out. He wrote to Joan to say that he wanted her to have one-third of his savings and that the remaining two-thirds should be divided between their disabled daughter (who would get the lion's share) and her two brothers. Harry died and was survived by Joan and their three children. Harry's letter did not amount to a valid will so that the intestacy rules applied to his estate. The operation of those rules resulted in Joan getting all Harry's money and their children nothing at all.

Case study 2

Freda left her husband George and their children to live with Adam. Freda never returned to her husband and family. George looked after the home, which belonged to him alone, and their children. He did not take any steps to end his marriage nor did he make a will. George died in an accident and was survived by Freda. Under the intestacy rules, Freda was entitled to George's personal belongings and the first £125,000 of his estate. She did not want the belongings but claimed the £125,000. This meant that George's house had to be sold; the children lost their home and were not left with very much.

Case study 3

James and Kathleen, who were not married to each other, lived together for 18 months in a house that belonged to James. They had twins and James also had three children from his marriage to Anne. James died without having made a will. Following his death, James's children, who were entitled to his estate under the intestacy rules, asked the courts to order Kathleen and her children to move out of the house so that it could be sold and the proceeds divided amongst them. Kathleen tried unsuccessfully to challenge their claim. The courts decided that Kathleen could remain in the house until the twins turned 21. The house would then have to be sold and the proceeds paid to James's children. Kathleen has virtually no means of her own and faces homelessness as she reaches 51.

Besides peace of mind, there are six good reasons for making a will.

1 Prevention of family strife

The failure to make a will can lead to confusion, disappointment and bitterness. An example of how this can arise is contained in Case Study 2.

2 Choice of personal representatives

You can choose your personal representatives who will deal with your estate when you die. If you die without having made a valid will, you have no say in the choice of your personal representatives who will be appointed by the courts according to statutory rules. They are usually persons who stand to inherit your estate under the intestacy rules. We use 'personal representatives' as an all-embracing expression to mean both executors (who are appointed by will) and administrators (who are appointed by the courts).

3 Choice of guardians

If you have children under the age of 18, you can appoint a guardian of your choice.

Most of the law about guardianship is contained in the Children Act 1989, which says that guardians may be appointed by will. This is an important consideration if you are the sole surviving parent of young children. The Act also says that the courts will appoint guardians of children under the age of 18 if their parents have made no appointments under their wills. We deal with the appointment of guardians in greater detail in Chapter 03.

4 Funeral arrangements

You can express your wishes about your funeral and the disposal of your body. We deal with these subjects in greater detail in Appendix 2.

5 Simplification

You can make the administration of your estate easier and probably cheaper to carry out by extending the powers of your executors and trustees.

6 Tax planning

Making a will can be a good opportunity for you to reduce the amount of tax payable on death. If you are happily married and the value of your joint estate is more than £500,000 you should give careful consideration to the use of Inheritance Tax saving measures. We look at these in Chapter 07.

Of course, not everyone needs to make a will. If you fall into any of the following categories, you may not need a will:

- The property you live in does not belong to you.
- The value of your savings and personal possessions is very small (say below £5,000). We deal with small estates in Chapter 17.
- You are one of those who are satisfied with the way that the intestacy rules apply to your estate. We deal with the intestacy rules in Chapter 13.
- The property you own will not pass under your will on your death. We look at this sort of property on pages 12–13.

Making a will is the only way you can be certain that your property goes where you want it to without paying more tax than is absolutely necessary.

02 who can make a will?

In this chapter you will learn:
- what a will is
- how old you have to be to make a will
- what is meant by being of sound mind
- whether or not an illiterate person or physically disabled person can make a will.

If you want to make a will, are aged 18 or over and are mentally capable, then there is no need to read the rest of this chapter. However, as with any legal matter, there are always some exceptions and difficulties and these are explained later in this chapter. Also before looking at these, let's make sure that you understand what a will is and some of the words used by lawyers.

2.1 What is a will?

A will is a formal declaration in writing by a person setting out what he or she wants to happen to their property after they die. Contrary to what many people believe, a will does not take effect until after the person dies. This means that it is possible for that person to change their mind (perhaps several times!) about who should inherit their property, and as a result make another will (or wills) before they die. If this happens, it is basically the last will that counts when the person dies. Another name for a will is a testament and the legal name for the person making it is a testator. Strictly speaking testator applies to a male will-maker and the term testatrix applies to a female will-maker. Throughout this book we use the term testator to apply to both.

There are just two basic qualifications for a person to make a will:

- they must be at least 18 years old
- they must be 'of sound mind'.

2.2 Age of testator

The key date is the day of your eighteenth birthday. On that day you can legally make a will. There is no upper age limit. So long as a person is of sound mind in the eyes of the law, they can make a will. This is true even for people who are over 100 years old.

2.2.1 Exceptions

The limit of 18 years old does not apply to those in the armed forces who are on active duty or to sailors who are at sea at the time they make their will. For these groups the law allows anyone over the age of 14 to make a will. The age of 14 may seem rather low, but it comes from a rule in the nineteenth century when the school leaving age was much lower. Today, for the purposes of making a will, the rule will really only apply to those aged 16 and 17. However, it may be necessary to decide if a will made many years ago is valid. For example, in 1938, a 15-year-old sailor might have made a will while at sea. Some 65 or more years later that sailor (now retired and aged 80 or so) could die without ever having changed that original will. In those circumstances the age limit would be important as that will made in 1938 could be a legally effective will.

The rule about lower age limits only applies to wills made by those in the armed forces who are on active duty. This does not mean that there need actually be a war, though clearly such situations as the Iraq War or the Gulf War would count as being on 'active service'. The courts have also decided that the rule covers situations such as troops on duty in Northern Ireland when there was terrorist activity. For sailors the key fact is that they must be 'at sea' when they make their will, if they wish to make one while under the age of 18 years.

2.3 Being of sound mind

The important point here is whether the person who wishes to make a will has sufficient mental capacity to understand that they are making a will and what effect it will have. So someone suffering from mental illness may be able to make a valid will. It depends on the severity of the mental illness and the mental capacity of the person at the time that they make the will.

Where a person has a retarded intellect, it is unlikely that they will be considered as having sufficient understanding. However, many people who suffer from mental illness may still be considered by the law as being of sound mind for the purpose of making a will. The key time is the moment at which they sign the will. If at that time they are capable of understanding that they are making a will and what effect it will have, then the will is valid.

This rule about being 'of sound mind' also applies to those suffering from physical illness. There are situations in which a physical illness means that the sufferer is taking such high doses of pain killing drugs that, whilst affected by those drugs, they are not capable of fully understanding what they are doing.

2.3.1 Advice

If there is any doubt about a person's mental capacity to make a will, then it is advisable to ask the doctor treating that person whether, in his opinion, they are capable of understanding the implications of making a will. But be warned that, even if the doctor says the person has the necessary mental capacity, there is no guarantee that the courts will accept that will as being validly made.

2.4 Illiteracy

Although the testator has to be able to understand what he or she is doing when they make a will, there is no requirement that they are capable of reading the will. Someone who cannot read or write may make a valid will by dictating their wishes to another person to write down. The testator does not even have to be able to write their own name. The law allows them to 'make their mark', usually by making a cross, instead of signing the will.

2.5 Physical disability

Physical disability does not prevent a person from making a valid will. If the testator is capable of making their wishes understood, then even those with very severe disabilities can make a will. For example, if someone has been paralyzed and is unable to sign, they may still make a will. Equally a person who is blind may make a will. In these cases the law allows the testator to tell another person to sign the will, but that signing must take place in the testator's presence.

03 preparing to make a will

In this chapter you will learn:
- to consider what your assets are
- to consider who should be your executors
- about appointing trustees
- about appointing guardians
- to consider who gets what.

In this chapter, we look at the steps you need to take if you have not previously made a valid will. If you have a will already and only want to make minor changes to it, a codicil may be the best way of doing this. (We deal with codicils in Chapter 09).

We suggest you now arm yourself with pen and paper and consider what follows:

3.1 What are my assets?

You should make a list of everything you own. You may find it helpful to complete the checklist on page 191.

There are some types of property that you cannot leave under your will. These are explained next.

3.1.1 Property outside your estate

At the end of Chapter 01, we said that there are some types of property whose future ownership does not depend upon what you say in your will. If you own property of this sort you should not include it in your checklist. The following are examples of property outside your estate.

a Nominated property

The law used to allow a person to dispose of deposits of money held by certain specific bodies by nominating who was to receive the money on death. This is generally no longer possible. Nominations made before this change in the law still work.

You are still allowed to nominate sums of up to £5,000 held by certain bodies such as friendly societies and industrial and provident societies.

b Insurance policies

It is quite common these days for a person to take out an insurance policy on his life for the benefit of someone else. In these circumstances, the policy monies do not belong to the person whose life is assured but to the other person. On the death of the life assured, the policy matures and the insurance company will pay the policy monies to the beneficiary. If there is a conflict between the terms of the policy and the will of the life assured, the terms of the policy will prevail and overrule the will.

c Pension benefits

Many people now belong to a pension scheme that provides for the payment of a lump sum by the trustees of the scheme to members of the employee's family if the employee dies while carrying out his job. Such payments do not belong to the employee and pass to his next of kin.

d Property held as a trustee for someone else

This is best illustrated by the following example.

Example

Christine and David are married and have three grandchildren. Five years ago, David put some money into a trust to meet the cost of his grandchildren's university education. David appointed Christine and himself to be the trustees of this trust. Christine and David should not include the trust monies in the checklist because these 'belong' to their grandchildren.

3.1.2 Jointly-owned property

You need to distinguish between property owned by joint owners for their own use and benefit and by joint owners for the use and benefit of someone else.

For all practical purposes, there are two sorts of legal ownership of joint property. One is known as a joint tenancy and the other as a tenancy in common. This distinction is important.

a Joint tenancies

A joint tenancy exists where two or more persons own property upon terms that give them identical interests in the whole of it. On the death of one joint tenant, the ownership of the entire interest in the property passes automatically to the surviving joint tenants.

Example

Christine and David own their family home as joint tenants. Christine dies before David and so David becomes the sole owner of the whole of the house.

---

b Tenancies in common

A tenancy in common exists where two or more persons own property upon terms that give each of them a share in it. In these circumstances, each person may sell or dispose of their share by will. If a tenant in common dies without having made a valid will, his share will pass in accordance with the intestacy rules. The share of one tenant in common can never pass automatically on death to the other tenants in common.

Example

Christine and David bought their family home for £300,000. Christine contributed £100,000 towards the purchase price and David £200,000. They own their home as tenants in common, Christine having a one-third share and David having a two-thirds share. By her will, Christine leaves everything she owns to David upon the condition that he survives her. Christine dies before David. On her death, David becomes the sole owner of the whole of the family home.

If Christine had not made a valid will, the position on her death would have been different. The family home would have been owned jointly by David, who would continue to have his two-thirds share and by Christine's personal representatives, who would have her one-third share. This situation could have serious implications for David. We look at the working of the intestacy rules in Chapter 13.

3.2 Who will be my executors?

In Chapter 01, we saw that an important reason for making a will is that you can chose those whom you want to carry out your wishes by appointing executors. There is no legal restriction on the number of executors you can appoint although the law allows a maximum of four to be named on the grant of probate. Most people appoint two executors. The more executors there are, the longer the administration of your estate is likely to take to complete and the more costly it may become.

You should be confident that the people you chose will be up to the job. If, for example, you own and run your own business successfully you may want to appoint someone with experience of that type of business who can keep it running as a going concern until a buyer can be found for it. Don't forget, either, to check with the persons you chose that they are willing and able to act.

If you are uncertain who to appoint, consider the following categories:

3.2.1 Friends or relatives

There is nothing in law to prevent a beneficiary under a will also being an executor. In practice, such arrangements can work well provided that there is no conflict of interest or antagonism between the executor/beneficiary and the other beneficiaries.

3.2.2 Professional advisers

Unlike a friend or a relative, a professional adviser such as a solicitor or an accountant will always want to be able to charge for their services. You will need, therefore, to balance the cost of administration against the advantage of placing the winding up of your estate in the hands of an expert.

3.2.3 Banks

Many banks provide a comprehensive administration service. Fees vary and it is important that you find out what the bank's charges are going to be before you make the appointment. Generally speaking, a bank's charges for winding up an estate will exceed those of a solicitor or accountant.

3.2.4 The Public Trustee

If you are completely stuck, you may be able to appoint the Public Trustee. He is a public officer whose duties are laid down by Act of Parliament. There are certain things that the Public Trustee cannot do such as run a charitable or religious trust or manage a business. The Public Trustee is entitled to be paid in accordance with a statutory scale of fees, which varies from time to time. If you are thinking of appointing the Public Trustee, you should contact his office (see p. 197).

3.3 Should I appoint trustees?

There is a technical distinction between an executor and a trustee, which we do not need to explain in this book. Usually, there is no reason why the same person should not be both an executor and a trustee of your will.

You need to appoint trustees if you create a trust in your will. You will need a trust if you want to leave some or all of your property to beneficiaries under the age of 18 or create a life interest for someone. We look at the subject of trusts in greater detail in Chapter 06.

3.4 Should I appoint guardians?

If you have young children, you should consider the appointment of a guardian to look after them until they reach 18. If you are the only surviving parent and have the care of your children, appointing a guardian is particularly important. If you are married and living with the other parent, you may wish to name guardians in case both of you die together. If you are separated from the other parent, it is advisable to get legal advice about the appointment.

As in the case of choosing executors and trustees, you should check with the proposed guardians that they are willing and able to act.

The duties of a guardian are quite extensive and costly. Guardians appointed under a will have no automatic legal right to be paid for caring for your children. You should consider making arrangements to cover the costs of the children's upbringing. We look at how this can be done in Chapter 06.

3.5 Deciding who gets what

English law upholds the principle that a person may dispose of his property to whom he likes. This principle applies both during the person's lifetime and on his death. Sometimes, this results in great hardship for a person who was financially dependent upon the deceased but, for whatever reason, is cut out of the will. Parliament recognized this and the current legislation dealing with disinheritance is contained in the Inheritance (Provision for Family and Dependants) Act 1975. This allows certain categories of claimant to challenge the will on the ground that they had been left out of it unjustifiably. We look at this Act in greater detail in Chapter 14.

In our experience, most people have a clear idea about where they want their property to go when they die. But if you are struggling, the following suggestions may be helpful to you:

- Draw up a list of all actual and potential beneficiaries. Include alternatives in case a primary beneficiary dies before you do. Where will their share go in those circumstances?

- Who are your primary beneficiaries? For most people it is their partner and/or children. What do you want them to inherit? Again, for most people it is the lion's share of their estate. So, if you are happily married, it is likely that you will want your spouse to be as comfortable and as secure as your circumstances allow.

- Always include alternative beneficiaries of major gifts in case a primary beneficiary dies before you or at the same time as you. Say what you want to happen to your property in the event of a major catastrophe such as a car accident in which you, your partner and any children are killed or if there are no surviving members of the generation above yours. In these circumstances, a gift to a charity of your choice might well be appropriate.

- After consulting your checklist, are there any particular items (for example, jewellery or books) that you want to leave to particular beneficiaries? Consider small gifts of cash to young members of the family, godchildren or nephews and nieces.

- If you and/or your spouse are worth a lot of money, consider Inheritance Tax saving schemes. We deal with this subject in Chapter 07.

04

how to make a will

In this chapter you will learn:
- whether or not it is necessary to go to a solicitor
- what sort of form to use and where to get a blank will form
- how to word do-it-yourself wills.

After reading the first three chapters and considering your assets and who you want to benefit, you are now ready to decide whether to make your own will or whether it is sensible to seek expert advice.

4.1 Is it necessary to go to a solicitor?

Generally, if you want to make an uncomplicated will, it is quite possible to write your own will without going to a solicitor. However, there are certain factors that may make it sensible to get legal advice. Check whether you come into any of the categories below.

4.1.1 Owning certain types of property

You should seriously think about getting legal advice if you have any property that comes under the following headings:

- large estate (over £350,000) as there may be benefits from estate-planning (see Chapter 07)
- shares in a private family company
- agricultural land
- income from a trust
- property abroad.

4.1.2 Business or investment involvement

You should take legal advice if you are:

- a partner or
- involved in any Lloyd's underwriting syndicate.

4.1.3 Lifetime gifts

Have you made large gifts during your lifetime or are you intending to do so in the future? This can complicate matters as certain gifts made within the seven years before death may be liable to Inheritance Tax. If you have made (or wish to make) gifts, then it is sensible to take advice.

4.1.4 Domiciled in another country

Are you are likely to be classed as being domiciled in another country outside the UK? For legal purposes 'domiciled' does not mean the same as 'reside'. If your parents were not British and/or you were born in another country, then even if you are presently residing in Britain, there is a possibility that you may be legally considered as domiciled in another country. The key question is whether you intend the United Kingdom to be your permanent home. If you intend to return to your country of origin at some time in the future, then you are probably not domiciled in Britain.

Example

Ibram, aged 49, came to England from Pakistan 10 years ago. He has lived in England since then, but has always said that he intends to return to Pakistan when he retires. For legal purposes Ibram will be regarded as domiciled in Pakistan. This complicates any will he makes as the law of England and Wales applies to the house he owns, but the law of Pakistan will apply to his savings.

4.1.5 Is your will going to be complicated?

If you have decided that you want to set up a trust in your will then legal advice is almost essential. If there are other complications, for example you want to leave parts of your estate to various people jointly, then it may be sensible to check that your intentions are clear. The more complicated you want to make your will, the more necessary legal advice becomes.

4.1.6 Deciding to do-it-yourself

Consider all the points above. If you decide that you wish to make your own will, then the next point is the practical one of what form is needed.

4.2 What sort of form to use and where to get a blank will form

The basic principle is that a will must be written. Video wills are not legally effective. However, what you write your will on does not matter. It does not even have to be paper. In one extreme case, a will was written on an eggshell.

It is possible to start from scratch and do the whole will yourself. It is also possible to buy will forms, which have key words printed at the beginning and at the end of the form, with gaps for you to fill in.

4.2.1 Using a will form

These can be obtained over the Internet or from most stationers, usually as part of a pack that contains two blank forms and gives brief explanations about making a will. There are also three sample wills in Appendix 01 on p. 179 of this book. The advantages of using one of these are, first, the heading is already printed in and it is easy to see where to fill in your own name and address at this point. There is also a part appointing executor(s) with spaces for you to fill in names and addresses. Finally, at the bottom of the sheet of paper there are clear places for you and the witnesses to sign.

The main disadvantage is that the form may not be long enough, particularly if you want to leave gifts to several different people, and it may be necessary to use an extra piece of paper. In this case it is necessary to make sure that the signing part at the bottom of the will form is crossed out and not used. Instead the same wording, together with the signatures of you and your witnesses, must appear on the last sheet at the end of the will.

4.2.2 Do-it-yourself

If you are not going to use a ready-made will form, then make sure the paper you use is blank without anything already written on it. It is also sensible to use good quality paper, which will stay in good condition for several years (after all you hope that you are not going to die too soon after making the will).

There is no set form of words for the start of a will but it is important to make clear who is making the will. If you have previously made a will, it is also important to make it clear that this new will is replacing the old will. After this, the next part should state who the executor(s) of the will are to be. An example of how to write these starting parts of the will is given opposite.

Example

THIS WILL is made by me .... [1]

of .... [2]

I revoke all previous wills and codicils I have made. I declare this will to be my last Will.

I appoint .... [3]

of .... [4]

and .... [5]

of .... [6]

to be the executors(s) of my Will.

[1] Print your full name here
[2] Write your full address here
[3] Print the first executor's full name here
[4] Write the first executor's full address here
[5] Print the second executor's full name here
[6] Write the second executor's full address here

Note **a** Generally speaking, you only need to appoint one executor but it is advisable to appoint at least two; **b** If you wish to appoint more than two executors, the extra names and addresses must be added after those of the second executor.

Advice on who to choose as your executors has already been given in Chapter 03.

4.3 How to word do-it-yourself wills

Apart from the start of the will, the wording largely depends on what property you are leaving and to whom. There are some general points: in particular, keep the wording simple and do not try to use legal jargon which may not mean what you think it means. It is important that the will expresses your wishes clearly. It is also sensible to keep to a logical order. The order we suggest, after the start and the appointment of executors, is:

- appointment of trustees (if necessary)
- appointment of guardians (if necessary)

- gifts of specified items of property (if any)
- general legacies
- dealing with the residue (the remainder of the estate)
- powers of executors and trustees.

The final part should be the signatures of the testator and the witnesses.

4.3.1 Preliminary matters

All wills should name the executors, but there are other points which may also apply to you, which should be dealt with at the start of the will, immediately after appointing the executors. These are:

a Trustees

If you wish to leave all or part of your estate in trust, then it is necessary to name the persons you wish to be trustees. It is sensible to check with these people that they are prepared to act as trustees. In the will state the names of those you are appointing as trustees and after their names write their address. (This is always a way of making sure that the identity of the person is clear.) The same people may be both executors and trustees. The wording should be:

> **Example**
>
> 'As trustees I appoint.................................(name)
>
> of ....(address)
>
> and ....(name)
>
> of ....(address)'

The powers of trustees are mentioned at the end of Chapter 06.

b Guardians

If you have young children, you may wish to appoint someone to act as their guardian. You can only do this if you have parental responsibility. If you are the only surviving parent and have the care of the children, appointing a guardian is particularly important. If you are married and living with the other parent, you may wish to name guardians in case both you and your partner die in the same accident or within a short time of each other. If you are separated from the other parent, then it is advisable to get legal advice on this point.

It is sensible to check with the people that they are prepared to be guardians if needed. Make sure their names and addresses are clearly written. If you are the only surviving parent then the wording is similar to that used for executors and trustees.

Example

'As guardians of my children I appoint:

....(name)

of ....(address)

and ....(name)

of ....(address)'

However, if both parents are alive at the time the will is being made, it is necessary to use different wording. For married couples, the words should be:

'If my wife/husband (name) dies before me or does not survive me for thirty days then as guardians of my children I appoint:...............................'

c Funeral wishes

If you have any particular wishes, these may be set out in your will. For example, you may put:

'I wish the remains of my body to be cremated.'

Many people want parts of their body to be used, if possible, in a transplant operation. This is best arranged by holding a donor card and making sure your nearest relatives know of your wishes. There is no need to repeat this wish in your will, though you can do so. If you only put these wishes in your will it may be too late to be of any use, as most transplant operations have to be carried out very quickly after death.

If you want your body to be used for medical research, you can include this wish in your will but it is also important to contact your nearest medical school or HM Inspector of Anatomy at the Department of Health. In addition, it is sensible to make sure your nearest relatives know of your wishes.

4.3.2 Main part of will

a Gifts

The main part of the will should set out each gift separately in a numbered list. The types of gift you can decide to leave are considered in the next chapter and examples of wording of the various different sorts are also set out there. As stated already, the most important rule is to use clear and simple language. Another point is clearly to identify each beneficiary, usually by giving their name and address. If they are related to you, then that relationship can also be stated to make identity clear.

b Legal clauses

There are also some legal clauses that we suggest are included to give your executors power to deal with your different kinds of property. This avoids problems as to exactly what they are allowed to do. The only time that you can safely leave these out is if you are leaving **everything** to **one** person who is **at least 18** years old.

(i) Powers to deal with your personal possessions (chattels)

The first power your executors need is to deal with all your personal possessions (legally called 'chattels'), which you have not specifically left to someone. If you look round your home, you will see that there is all the furniture and items such as clocks, vases, crockery, etc. All these are chattels. In addition there may be a car, TV, video, hi-fi equipment, personal computer, paintings and books. Then there is all the clothing, watches, jewellery ... The list is almost endless. The bigger items you will probably want to leave to certain people, but it is not practical to identify and list in your will all the items you own. Apart from anything else the exact items will change from time to time, as you buy new things and/or get rid of old things.

You may decide that you want to leave all your 'chattels' to one person; this is especially true if you are married. Or you may decide to leave certain items to individuals and all the rest to one person. It is also possible to leave a letter stating your wishes that certain items should go to certain people. This allows you to change your mind without the need for writing a new will, but you must realize that a letter of wishes is not legally binding and these wishes may not get carried out after your death.

However, you may prefer to let your executors deal with the chattels and in this case your executors need to have the power to do this and we suggest that the following clause should be included in your will.

Example

I give to my Executors absolutely, free of inheritance tax, all my personal chattels as defined by section 55(1) (x) of the Administration of Estates Act 1925.

I request my Executors, without imposing any trust or binding obligation upon or conferring any interest upon any other person, to dispose of my personal chattels in accordance with any letter of wishes of mine that may come to their attention within six (6) months of my death.

This gets over any problems of items you forgot to mention specifically in your will. It also prevents any difficulties over new items that have been bought since you made your will. It asks your executors to respect any known wishes and should prevent disputes between beneficiaries as to who is going to have the TV, etc.

(ii) Powers to deal with other property

If you own or lease a house, flat or other land, then it may be necessary for this property to be sold after you die. It is also necessary to make sure that other assets such as money in a bank or building society account, stocks and shares are easily transferred and, where needed, sold to raise money. Again, you may leave certain property to a particular person. For example, if you are married, it is quite probable that you wish to leave your house (or your share of the house, if it is jointly owned) to your husband or wife. Another example is that you may decide to leave all the shares you own to your son or daughter. However, there may be situations where you want some property to be divided between two (or more) people. Also, you may move house or change your investments and you do not want to have to keep changing your will.

For these reasons we advise that you include the following clause in your will:

Example

I give all my real and personal property of every kind which is not disposed of by my Will or any codicil to it to my Executors. My Executors must hold this property upon trust to:

- sell the whole or any part of it; or
- keep the whole or any part of it in the same form as it was at the date of my death for as long as my Executors decide.

The decision of my Executors whether to sell or to keep my property is a matter for them alone and they will not be liable for any loss caused as a result of the exercise of their discretion.

The aim of this is to prevent family squabbles over what should be done, and also protects the executors. For example, they may decide not to sell your shares immediately and then the value of the shares goes down suddenly. This clause stops anyone from claiming that the executors should personally be liable for the loss of value of the shares.

(iii) Powers to pay expenses, debts, taxes and legacies

Your executors will have to pay out sums of money for various matters such as funeral expenses and debts. They will also have to pay costs of dealing with your will, including any tax due on your estate, and pay all legacies to the appropriate beneficiaries. In order to make sure there are no problems over their rights to do this, you should state all this in your will.

Example

My Executors must pay out of the monies arising from such sale:

- my funeral expenses
- any testamentary expenses
- any debts
- any legacies, and
- any taxation payable by reason of my death.

4.3.3 The end of the will

Finally the will has to be signed and witnessed. This should be done in ink. Strictly speaking the testator can sign anywhere in the will, but it is better to make matters clear by signing at the end. Immediately before the testator's signature, the date should be written. Then comes an important statement called the 'attestation clause', after which the witnesses should sign (rules on who can be a witness are given in Chapter 08). The words for the attestation clause are a statement that the witnesses and the testator were all present when each of them signed. The words we use for this are: 'Signed by the testator/testatrix in our joint presence and then by us together in his/hers'. Finally the witnesses must sign the will.

There is more detail on how to witness a will in Chapter 08, with a checklist to make sure this important part is done correctly.

In Appendix 01 there are examples of wills, in which you can see how all these parts link together.

05

gifts

In this chapter you will learn:
- about different types of gifts in a will
- how gifts can 'fail' and what can be done to prevent this from happening
- about making gifts to children under 18
- about making gifts to charities.

5.1 Different types of gift

Gifts in a will are sometimes referred to by their technical names. A 'devise' is a gift of land and a 'legacy' is a gift of something other than land, such as your personal possessions, money, shares and so on. This technical distinction is not one we will refer to in this chapter. Instead, we will speak simply of 'gifts' and 'gifting'. For practical purposes, there are only two categories of gift: gifts of specific items and gifts of a general (or non-specific) nature.

5.1.1 Specific gifts

A specific gift is a gift of a particular item or number of items of property that the testator owns. The gift may be of land or something other than land. Whatever the subject matter may be, it is important to describe the gift as accurately and as clearly as possible. If you do not do this, your gift may not end up where you want it to because your executors will not be certain which item you are talking about. In these circumstances, the law says that the gift 'fails'. We look at what happens when this occurs later in section 5.2 of this chapter.

Examples

A   Ursula, a widow without children, owns a collection of rings and brooches. She decides to leave them to her sister, Veronica. Ursula's will contains the following clause: 'I give the whole of my collection of rings and brooches to my sister Veronica provided that she survives me'. Veronica outlives Ursula and inherits all the rings and brooches as Ursula intended.

B   Quentin, a married man, decides to leave £10,000 to his best friend. His will contains the following clause: 'I give £10,000 to my friend, Pauline Brown of 72 Hartland Road Cornford Loamshire provided that she survives me'. Pauline outlives Quentin and inherits £10,000.

C   Henry, a single man, enjoys music and has a valuable collection of records, which he decides to divide between his two best friends. His will contains the following clauses 'I give (a) my pop records to my good friend Jack Smith of 37 High Road Cornford Loamshire and (b) my easy listening records to my friend Kathleen Brown of Flat B Mulberry Court Mulberry Road North Ham London SE29'. Henry's executors

are unable to distinguish between his 'pop records' and his 'easy listening records' because it appears to them that all the records fall into both categories. The gifts fail and Jack and Kathleen are disappointed.

D Alec, a widower and a farmer, owns several pieces of land in the same area. One consists of fields and another of water meadows. He decides to give the fields to his son, Richard and the water meadows to his daughter, Susan. He describes each piece of land carefully following the descriptions contained in the title deeds. As a result, Richard and Susan get what their father intended.

5.1.2 Non-specific gifts

A non-specific gift is a gift of something general such as 'all my personal possessions' or '1,000 shares in PQR Limited'. You will see from these examples that there is no indication that any specific items or shares are intended to be gifted.

5.1.3 Residuary gifts

In the same way that we have distinguished between a specific gift and a non-specific gift, you should be aware of the difference between a gift of residue (a residuary gift) and a gift of something other than residue (a non-residuary gift).

Example

Frederick, a wealthy married man with four children, gives £200,000 to his executors to put into trust for his children. He also gives several personal possessions to his close friends. Everything else he leaves to his wife upon the condition that she survives him by 28 days. The gifts of money and personal possessions are non-residuary gifts and the gift of everything else to his wife is a gift of residue.

---

a What is 'residue'?

Residue is the term used to refer to all the property of the testator that has not been given away by his will. Such property is usually called the testator's 'residuary estate'.

The distinction between residue and non-residue is important for several reasons. The principal one is that you need to be certain that your residuary estate passes to your beneficiaries in the way you want. Also, you need to avoid a situation in which your will does not dispose of some part of your property which is capable of passing under your will. The technical expression for this situation is 'partial intestacy'. You will find an illustration in the example below.

Example

George, a wealthy bachelor, divides his estate equally between his three friends Peter, Quentin and Rosalind. George's will does not say what is to happen to his property if one (or more) of his friends dies before him. Quentin is killed ten months before George dies of natural causes. On George's death, his estate is divided into three equal shares. Peter and Rosalind inherit their one-third shares. The remaining one-third share passes in accordance with the intestacy rules. (This result would have been avoided if George's will had said what was to happen if Quentin died before him.)

---

b What happens to the residue?

Your residuary estate is usually the source of the funds used to pay:

- your debts
- your funeral and testamentary expenses
- any legacies, and
- sometimes, but not always, Inheritance Tax.

In our model forms of will, all these items are stated to be payable out of residue.

The structuring of a gift of residue is important. This will usually depend upon who the residuary beneficiary is. To put that another way, will the residuary beneficiary acquire the gift immediately after your death or not? In the case of a gift of residue to a beneficiary under 18, there can be no immediate acquisition, which means that you must create a trust to hold the gift on behalf of the beneficiary until he reaches 18 (or some other higher age). We look at what trusts are and how they work in greater detail in Chapter 06.

When you intend the residuary beneficiary to inherit immediately, he or she will assume control over the property there and then. It is important not to overlook the implications of this. If the residuary beneficiary dies a few days after you (perhaps as a result of injuries received in an accident in which you were involved) your gift to him will end up in the hands of the beneficiaries of his will, if he has made one, or those who inherit under the intestacy rules, if he has not. In our experience, most testators like to exert a degree of control over their property so that, if the principal beneficiary dies within a short time of the testator, a substitute beneficiary inherits instead.

We shall now look at the subject of survivorship and substitution in greater detail and illustrate the workings of survivorship and substitutional clauses (pages 34–7).

5.2 Failure of gifts by will

5.2.1 Death of a beneficiary

Besides taking care to describe the subject matter of your gift properly, you must also consider what you want to happen to the gifted property if the beneficiary of it dies before you.

Generally speaking, if a beneficiary dies before the testator, the gift will fail.

It often happens that a beneficiary of a gift under a will dies before the testator. What happens in those circumstances depends on whether the gift is one of residue or not. (We explained what residue is on page 32.)

a Non-residuary beneficiary

If the beneficiary is not a residuary beneficiary, the gift becomes part of the testator's residuary estate.

Example

By her will, Helen gives £5,000 to her friend Mary and leaves everything else to her husband, Jack. Mary dies before Helen. Helen then dies before Jack. The gift to Mary fails. The £5,000 becomes part of Helen's residuary estate, which passes to Jack.

---

b Residuary beneficiary

If the recipient of the gift is a beneficiary of the residuary estate, the gift will pass under the intestacy rules.

> ### Example
>
> By her will Ursula, a widow without children, divides everything she owns equally between her friend Veronica, and sister Wilhemina. Ursula's will does not say what is to happen to these shares if Veronica and/or Wilhemina dies before her. Wilhemina dies six months before Ursula who, curiously, does not change her will. Veronica outlives Ursula. On Ursula's death, one-half of her estate passes to Veronica. The other half is dealt with under the intestacy rules and, as Ursula has no other relations, passes to the Crown.

5.2.2 Alternative or substitute beneficiaries

To make sure that your property goes where you want it to, you should include alternative or substitute beneficiaries wherever possible. This can be done quite simply by making the gift conditional upon the primary beneficiary surviving you by a specified period and then saying what is to happen to the gifted property if he does not. Such an arrangement is known technically as a 'survivorship clause'. The survival period should be neither too long (otherwise it will hold up the administration of the estate) nor too short. Twenty-eight days is quite usual and we use that period in this book. If we look again at the last example, Ursula could have made the gifts to Veronica and Wilhemina conditional upon each of them surviving her by 28 days and going on to say that, if one of them did not, the other would inherit the whole of her estate, as in the next example.

> ### Example
>
> By her will, Ursula, a widow without children, divides her estate equally between her friend, Veronica, and her sister, Wilhemina. The gifts to Veronica and Wilhemina are conditional upon each of them surviving Ursula by 28 days. If one of them does not satisfy that condition, her share passes to the other. If both of them fail to survive the 28-day period, the whole of Ursula's estate goes to charity. Wilhemina dies six months before Ursula. Veronica outlives Ursula and inherits the whole of Ursula's estate.

5.2.3 What if two (or more) people die at the same time?

There is another reason why survivorship clauses are important. Unlike Scotland, the law in England and Wales does not recognize, for the purposes of inheriting property under a will, that two people can die at the same time. If there is no evidence of the order of death (for example, in the case of a car crash) the law says that the older person is treated as having died before the younger one. This rule relates only to inheriting property under a will. It does not apply to the intestacy rules or to Inheritance Tax law where in both cases the deceased and the beneficiary are treated as having died at the same time.

5.2.4 Testator's children as beneficiaries

There is yet another special rule in the case of gifts made by a testator to his children. It applies to both residuary and non-residuary gifts unless the will says or shows otherwise. The rule is that, where a testator leaves property to a child of his who dies before him, leaving a child who survives the testator, the grandchild takes the share of the testator's estate that his parent would otherwise have taken.

Example

By his will James, a married man with two children, leaves all his property to his wife Kathleen provided she survives him by 28 days but if she does not, then equally between his two children, Alan aged 29 and Bethan aged 25. Alan is single and Bethan is married with a young son. James, Kathleen and Bethan die in a road accident. Under his will, James's property is divided equally between Alan and James's grandson.

As we have said, there is an important qualification to this rule. It applies only if the will does not say or show anything to the contrary. So, James could have said that, if Bethan does not survive him by 28 days, her share of his estate will pass to Alan. In those circumstances, Bethan's young son would receive nothing.

5.2.5 Leaving gifts to several people

Sometimes a testator wants to make a gift to more than one person or to a class of people such as godchildren, nephews or nieces. If this is not done properly, all sorts of complications can arise. The simplest way of doing this is to identify each of the beneficiaries by name and say what is to happen to the gift if one (or more) of them dies before you do.

Example

I give £500 to each of the following grandchildren of mine if they survive me by 28 days:

- Anne Brown, Bernadette Brown, Christine Brown and Delia Brown all of Flat B Mulberry Court Mulberry Road North Ham London SE29 and
- to Simon Smith, Roger Smith and Thomas Smith all of 37 High Road Cornford Loamshire.

5.2.6 The effect of divorce and annulment on gifts

The effect of the grant of a decree of dissolution (in other words, divorce) or annulment of marriage is to cancel any gift by will to a former spouse, unless the will says or shows otherwise. This is why anyone involved in divorce or annulment proceedings should always give serious consideration to making a new will.

5.3 Four things you need to know about gifting by will

5.3.1 Ademption

If you make a specific gift in your will of any sort of property which you then dispose of (for example, by giving it away, selling or destroying it) before you die, the disappointed beneficiary will have no claim against your estate. This principle is known technically as 'ademption.'

5.3.2 Beneficiaries beware

On pages 58–61 we will look in detail at the formalities that must be followed when the time comes to sign your will. One of these is that the will must be signed in the presence of two witnesses. Never ask a beneficiary or the spouse of a beneficiary to be a witness when you sign your will. If you do, the beneficiary cannot take the gift in the will.

5.3.3 Abatement

A common worry of testators is that there may not be enough money in their estates when they die to pay all the legacies after any debts and other liabilities have been settled. If this happens, the legacies are reduced. This is known technically as 'abatement'.

5.3.4 Personal possessions (or 'chattels')

The gifting of personal possessions can be a source of anxiety if the list of who is to get what changes; for example, because a beneficiary dies or a particular item is disposed of. Many testators nowadays find it convenient to gift personal possessions by reference to a letter of wishes addressed to their executors. The advantage of this arrangement is that, if you change your mind about who is to get what, all you need do is to write a new letter rather than draw up a new will. You will find a specimen letter of wishes at the end of this chapter.

We have said already that a letter of wishes is just that and no more; the law does not treat such letters as imposing a legal obligation on executors to carry out what they are asked to do in the letter. Because of this, some people feel more comfortable if they dispose of their personal possessions by means of specific gifts contained in their will.

5.4 Gifts to children under 18

The difficulty with making gifts by will to children is that, generally speaking, the law says a person under the age of 18 cannot give a valid receipt for property. The effect of this rule is that executors must usually retain the gifted property until the child reaches 18.

There is one way of softening the effect of this rule in relation to non-residuary gifts. This is to allow your executors to accept the receipt of the beneficiary's parent or guardian. This relieves your executors from all liability to the child beneficiary; it does not compel your executors to hand over the property to the child.

Example

'I give £500 to my grandson Simon Smith of 37 High Road Cornford Loamshire and if at the time of my death he has not attained the age of 18 years then the receipt of his parent or guardian will be a complete discharge to my Executors.'

Please also remember the special 'substitutional' rule we mentioned on page 35 when planning to make gifts to children.

5.5 Gifts to charities

If you want to make a gift to charity, there are three factors to bear in mind:

1 It is essential that the charity is accurately identified. The best way of doing this is to state its name, address and registration number. This information can be obtained from any reputable guide to charities available at your nearest public reference library or from the Charities Commission website.

2 Charities cease to exist for a number of reasons. If the charity is no longer in existence or has amalgamated with another charity at the time of your death, your gift will fail unless your executors are allowed to make the gift to another charity which, in their opinion, most nearly fulfils the objects of the original charity. If you have no objection to this arrangement, you can include a clause in your will in the following terms:

'If the charity is no longer in existence at the date of my death, the benefit of my gift shall be given to any other charity having the same or similar objects which my Executors in their absolute discretion decide.'

3 Your executors need to obtain a good receipt for the gift. It is essential, therefore, that you allow them to accept a receipt from the secretary or treasurer of the charity concerned. A suitable clause would be:

'The receipt of the person who appears to my Executors to be the treasurer or secretary of the charity to whom this gift is given will be a complete discharge to my Executors'.

---

30 September 2000

22 Main Street
Cornford
Loamshire

TO: Jeremy Watts and Veronica Strange

Dear Jeremy and Veronica

I have made my will today and have appointed you to be my Executors.

You will see that I ask you to dispose of my 'personal chattels' in accordance with any letter of wishes of mine which may come to your attention within three months of my death. Without seeking to impose any legal obligation upon you, I should like you to deal with my possessions in the following way:

1   I give to my good friend Adam Baines of 18 Tulip Close, Conford, Loamshire all my books and pictures.

2   I give to my good friend Christine Davies of Magnolia Cottage, 4 Oaks, Cornford, Loamshire all my jewellery.

3   I give to Elizabeth Fuggles of Flat C, 45 Newtown Close, Cornford, Loamshire my canteen of silver cutlery with grateful thanks for all the help she gave me.

To the extent that there may be personal chattels of mine not disposed of by this letter, I should like you to sell them as soon as possible and to add the proceeds to my residuary estate.

Yours ever
Ursula Bentham

---

figure 5.1 letter of wishes example

06

trusts

In this chapter you will learn:
- what a trust is
- whether a trust is necessary
- the different types of trust
- about trustees' powers
- about the relationship between trustees and beneficiaries.

In this chapter we look at what trusts are and how they can be of great help in the will-making process.

6.1 What is a trust?

A trust is a legal arrangement where one group of people called 'trustees' take responsibility for property for the benefit of another group of people called 'beneficiaries'. Trusts come into existence in all sorts of circumstances. A person can create a trust during their lifetime (when they are called the 'settlor') or on death by their will. Trusts are used nowadays for a multitude of things such as:

- To prevent assets, particularly family assets, from being wasted.
- To enable property (usually land) to be held for a child. The law says that a person under 18 is incapable of holding legal title to land. We also saw in Chapter 05 that a child cannot give a valid receipt for property to the testator's personal representatives.
- To provide pensions to former employees and others.
- To operate unit trusts and other similar investment vehicles.
- To save tax.

6.2 Is a trust necessary?

In the context of will making, it is not usually necessary to create a trust for a non-residuary gift. There is one exception to this to which we refer on page 44.

Broadly speaking, there are three situations where a trust is needed when considering a gift of residue.

6.2.1 Children

If you intend to make a residuary gift of any sort of property to a child, a trust is necessary because (as we have seen) the law does not allow a child to give a valid receipt to your personal representatives or to hold legal title to land.

Example

Patrick, a widower with two children, owns a house and investments. He decides to divide everything he owns equally between his son, Quentin, who is now 20 and his daughter, Ruth, who is now 15. If Patrick dies today, a trust will be needed to hold Ruth's share of his estate until she reaches 18.

Example

It is ten years later. Patrick's circumstances are unchanged except that he now has grandchildren. Quentin has married and has a young son and daughter. Ruth is still single. Patrick decides to divide everything he owns equally between Quentin and Ruth upon the condition that each of them survives him by 28 days. If Quentin does not survive Patrick by 28 days, Patrick's grandchildren (now 4 and 1 respectively) will inherit the share that their father would have taken. If Quentin and Ruth fail to survive Patrick by 28 days, Patrick's grandchildren will inherit their aunt's share as well as their father's share. A trust will be necessary in case Patrick's grandchildren inherit if their father and/or aunt do not outlive their grandfather by 28 days.

6.2.2 Life interests

Sometimes, a testator wants to tie up property in order to give one person, usually called 'the life tenant', the right to enjoy that property during their lifetime and, on their death, to make an outright gift of the property to someone else. The most common life interests are a right to occupy property as in Example A below or a right to receive income from investments as in Example B.

Example A

Michael, a retired teacher with three adult children, is married to Norma, who is several years younger than her husband. Michael owns the family home. He wants Norma to live there after his death for the rest of her life if she wants to and, on her death, for the property to be sold and the proceeds shared equally between their children. This can be achieved if Michael creates a trust giving Norma a life interest in the family home and requiring the trustees to sell it following her death and divide the net proceeds between the children.

Example B

Edward, a wealthy man in his own right is married to Freya who is also comfortably off. They have four children. By his will, Edward makes non-residuary gifts to his friends and others and divides his residuary estate into two parts: land and investments. He gives the land to Freya upon the condition that she survives him by 28 days. Everything else he puts into a trust under which the income from his investments is paid to Freya during her lifetime. On her death, the trust comes to an end, the investments being divided equally between those of his four children who are alive at the date of their mother's death.

6.2.3 Contingent interests

The interest of a beneficiary in property is called 'contingent' if his interest in or entitlement to that property is conditional upon the happening of an event. The following example illustrates this point.

Example

Susan, who is unmarried, wishes to leave everything she owns to her nephew Tom. Susan thinks that Tom will not be old enough to look after his inheritance until he reaches the age of 25. She therefore makes the gift to Tom conditional (or contingent) upon him reaching 25. If Susan dies before Tom has reached that age then his interest is contingent and her personal representatives must hold her property in trust until he attains the specified age of 25 or dies before then.

A contingent interest needs to be distinguished from a vested interest. The interest of a beneficiary in property is called 'vested' if his entitlement to that interest is immediate. The following example illustrates the difference between a contingent interest and a vested one.

> **Example**
>
> Charles, a widower with two adult children, decides to divide everything he owns equally between them. If they survive their father, the children will acquire vested interests in his estate. If Charles says that his children will not inherit unless they reach (say) 30, they will not have vested interests, but contingent ones.

So, if you decide to make a contingent gift, you will need to create a trust.

6.3 Different types of trust

There are many different types of trust. Generally speaking, will making is concerned with three sorts.

6.3.1 The discretionary trust

This is a trust under which the trustees have discretion about how the trust monies are to be used. Very often, the degree of discretion is wide so that who gets what is entirely a matter for the trustees. Discretionary trusts are a useful tax planning tool for married couples.

6.3.2 The accumulation and maintenance trust

This special sort of trust is suitable for making future financial provision for your children and grandchildren. Such trusts enjoy privileged Inheritance Tax status.

6.3.3 The interest in possession trust

So called, because this is a trust where the beneficiaries have a clear right to the use of trust property as in Examples A and B on pages 43 and 44.

6.4 Trustees' powers

If a trust is required, the trustees should have all the powers they need to enable them to carry out their duties efficiently. Trustees' powers (and their duties and obligations) come from three sources: Acts of Parliament (usually referred to as 'statutory powers'); general law (sometimes called 'common law powers') and the document creating the trust (usually known as 'express powers').

We approach the subject of appropriate powers for your trustees from the point of view that you will need to include some, perhaps all, of the following non-statutory provisions in your will.

6.4.1 Appropriation

Your personal representatives may use any part of your estate to do things like pay legacies provided that no particular beneficiary is prejudiced. The law provides that your personal representatives must obtain the consent of the beneficiaries before dealing with your estate in a particular way unless your will says otherwise. It is customary to say that your personal representatives do not need to obtain the consent of the beneficiaries.

Example

Felicity gives £10,000 to her best friend Gregory and everything else to her sister Harriet. Felicity's residuary estate includes some investments now worth £6,500 and cash of £3,500. Provided that Gregory consents, the shares can be appropriated to him in part satisfaction of his legacy, the balance being paid in cash.

Unless Felicity's will says otherwise, her personal representatives will need to obtain Gregory's consent to this arrangement.

6.4.2 Receipts for legacies to children

We dealt with this topic on pages 38–9.

6.4.3 Exclusion of apportionment rules

The law contains some very complicated rules relating to the apportionment of income to periods before and after the date of your death. It is customary nowadays to say that these rules do not apply and that instead all income received by your personal representatives will be treated as income at the date of receipt irrespective of the period for which it is payable.

Example

Peter's will contains a specific gift of shares to his friend Quentin. Following Peter's death, a dividend from these shares is paid to Peter's executors. The dividend relates to a period partly before and partly after his death. To whom does the dividend belong? The Apportionment Act 1870 provides an answer, albeit a complicated one. It is because of these complications that it is customary to say that income is deemed to be income at the date of its receipt.

6.4.4 Investment

Trustees' statutory powers relating to investment and the purchase of land have been overhauled by Parliament recently. The important things to remember are that trustees (and personal representatives) must review investments regularly and take proper advice (for example, from a stock broker) about how to deal with them.

6.4.5 Maintenance of a child

The law contains rather complicated technical rules about what trustees can and cannot do with income that they are holding for a child beneficiary. It is now common to allow your trustees to use income to benefit a child beneficiary in any way that your trustees think fit.

6.4.6 Advancement of capital

The law gives trustees (and personal representatives) power to make capital available to a beneficiary who has a vested or contingent interest in it, subject to certain conditions. Again, it is now common to allow your trustees to advance capital to such a beneficiary provided that your trustees are satisfied that the capital will be used for his benefit. On pages 182–4 there is an example of a will with trusts, showing how trustees' powers can be extended.

6.5 The relationship between trustees and beneficiaries

Trustees have what might be described as a general duty of good faith to the beneficiaries. Thus, trustees are obliged (amongst other things) to:

- take reasonable care of the trust property
- ensure all the beneficiaries are fairly treated
- act unanimously (unless the will says decisions may be taken and acted upon by a majority)
- consult the beneficiaries if the trustees hold land in trust (but not, for example, investments) and
- provide information and accounts to the beneficiaries.

Trustees are also prohibited from making any profit from their trust and charging for their services unless the will specifically allows this.

There is no legal prohibition on a beneficiary also being a trustee. This may not be appropriate in every case, for example if there is a dispute between the two groups.

6.6 Trusts and saving inheritance tax

We have said already that trusts can be a useful tool in tax planning for married couples. In Chapter 07, we will see how this works.

In this chapter you will learn:
- the basics of inheritance tax
- special rules for married couples and inheritance tax
- about business property relief
- about agricultural property relief.

What does 'estate planning' mean? We see estate planning as an exercise that results in the right balance for you being struck between tax saving considerations on the one hand and the preservation of your assets coupled with provision for your family and any dependants on the other hand. Sometimes this balance is difficult to achieve. If you find yourself in these circumstances, you should obtain professional advice.

We have made four technical assumptions in the examples contained in this chapter. These are that:

- everyone is domiciled in the United Kingdom for tax purposes
- no one has made a potentially exempt transfer (see page 52) within the last seven years
- everyone has used all the other exemptions and reliefs available to them for lifetime transfers, and
- the figures reflect the changes contained in the April 2003 Budget.

7.1 The basics of Inheritance Tax (IHT)

Inheritance Tax is in effect a tax on the transfer of wealth by one person to another. It is normally paid on death, although it can be paid during a person's lifetime. On death, it is charged on what amounts to the net value of the deceased's assets at the date of death. If that value exceeds a certain amount, IHT will be payable. It is paid on slices or 'bands' (as they are known technically) of your wealth, in the same way that Income Tax is payable at different rates or bands of your income. There are currently two bands of IHT. The first band is usually referred to by its technical name – the nil rate band – so called, because the rate of tax is 0%. This applies to the first £255,000 in value of a person's property. The second band applies where the value of the transfer of property exceeds £255,000 but only to the amount over that figure. The nil rate band is reviewed annually by Parliament and adjusted, usually in line with inflation.

IHT is currently payable at the rate of 40% for transfers on death and at 20% on lifetime transfers.

> **Example**
>
> Gwen, a widow, owns a house valued at £355,000 and has savings of £100,000. By her will, she leaves everything she owns to her sister, Harriet. At the date of her death, the value of Gwen's estate is £455,000. The first £255,000 in value is liable to IHT at the rate of 0%. The balance of £200,000 is liable to IHT at the rate of 40%, which gives rise to a tax bill of £80,000.

As we have said, IHT may be payable on lifetime transfers as well as on transfers on death. If IHT was only payable on death, people would try to avoid the tax by gifting away as much as possible during their lifetime. To stop this, IHT is charged on certain types of lifetime transfers if the person making the transfer dies within seven years of it.

7.1.1 Terminology of IHT

It is helpful to get a feel for the terminology of IHT. There are three key expressions you need to know: what a 'chargeable transfer' is and whether a transfer is 'exempt' or 'potentially exempt'.

a Chargeable transfers

Broadly speaking, a chargeable transfer is any sort of transfer (for example a gift or a sale) of any sort of property made by an individual that is not an exempt transfer. From this, we can see that IHT may be payable on some gifts and sales but not all of them made during a person's lifetime and on their death. Next, we need to distinguish between an 'exempt transfer' and a 'potentially exempt transfer'. An exempt transfer is a transfer of property where IHT will never be payable. A potentially exempt transfer (usually known as a PET) is one that may not be liable to IHT if certain conditions are satisfied.

b Exempt transfers

The most important categories of exempt transfers are:

* the nil rate band (see above)
* transfers between husband and wife
* gifts to charities, political parties and for national purposes.

Such transfers are always exempt, whether made on the death or during the lifetime of the transferor. The following are the most common exempt lifetime transfers:

- individual gifts of £250 each – you are currently allowed to make any number of gifts up to £250 each in any one tax year; and
- small gifts – you are currently allowed to give up to £3,000 in any one tax year to any number of individuals.

c Potentially exempt transfers (PETs)

A PET is a lifetime gift by one individual to another or to the trustees of certain types of trust that will never be liable to IHT provided that the transferor lives for more than seven years from the date of the gift. If the transferor dies within that seven-year period, IHT will be chargeable. The rate at which IHT is chargeable in these circumstances is 40% but the amount attributable to the gift may be reduced, depending on the number of years that have passed since the date of the gift. This is called 'tapering relief'.

Example

Quentin owns property to the value of £900,000. In October 2002, he gives £50,000 to his godson Robert. Quentin dies in January 2006, nearly 3 and a half years after the gift. IHT is charged at the rate of 40% but the resulting figure is reduced by 20%.

Common examples of PETs are:

- gifts of money by grandparents to grandchildren;
- the creation of an accumulation and maintenance trust (see Chapter 06); and
- gifts of land by one person to another.

You will now understand the basic principles of IHT and how it works. In Chapter 19, we will explain the steps involved in calculating IHT on death; how to do the sums and who is liable to pay.

7.2 Married couples and IHT

7.2.1 Introduction

For many years, Parliament singled out married couples for special tax treatment. Married couples used to enjoy significant tax advantages that other couples who were not married to each other did not. Many of those privileges (for example, the married person's income tax allowance) have been eroded. In the case of IHT, there is still no liability on the transfer of property by one spouse to the other if both spouses are domiciled in the UK.

It remains to be seen how long this preferential arrangement will last. Those who maintain that there is no longer any justification for married couples to be treated differently from other couples have influenced the tax treatment of married couples for several years recently. But, for the (happily) married couple with a family who have acquired some wealth, the current state of the law provides a means of saving a significant amount of IHT.

7.2.2 The use of the nil rate band

The amount of IHT payable on the death of the second spouse can be significantly reduced if both spouses make wills that provide for an amount equal to their respective nil rate bands to pass to beneficiaries other than the surviving spouse. If the result of that arrangement is to leave insufficient property to the surviving spouse, the testator could create a discretionary trust to use up the nil rate band for the benefit of the surviving spouse and the other beneficiaries so that personal needs of the surviving spouse can take precedence over tax savings if circumstances require.

Example

Christine and David own their house valued at £450,000 and have savings (including investments) of £500,000. Together they are worth £950,000. They have three adult children and six grandchildren. By her will, Christine gives property to the value of £255,000 to her three children; everything else she leaves to David. David also makes his will along the same lines. Christine dies first and is survived by David and their children. On Christine's death, no IHT is payable because the gift to her children is exempt (being within the nil rate band) as is the gift to her husband (being a transfer between spouses). After Christine's death, David changes his will to leave everything to his three children. On his death, David's estate is worth £695,000. IHT of £176,200 is payable, calculated as follows:

Gross estate	£695,000
Less nil rate band	£255,000
Taxable estate	£440,000
IHT at 40% of £440,000	£176,200
Amount available for children (who already have £255,000 under Christine's will)	£518,800

If Christine had given £255,000 to David and not to her children, David's gross estate would have been £950,000 with the result that IHT of £278,000 would have been payable on David's death. By using her nil rate band in the way Christine did, Their family saved inheritance tax of £101,800.

7.2.3 The family home

It often happens that the family home is owned jointly by husband and wife and represents a large, if not the largest, asset of the family. Ideally, the family home should not be taken account of in a tax planning exercise but this may be hard to achieve in practice.

We saw in Chapter 03 that property held by two (or more) people may be owned by them as joint tenants or as tenants in common. You will remember that property owned by joint tenants passes automatically to the survivor on death but that property owned by tenants in common does not. So, if you and your spouse own the family home as joint tenants, the survivor of you will own the property outright on first death. On the other hand, if you own the family home as tenants in common, your share will pass according to what you say in your will.

If you are a tenant in common of the family home, to whom do you leave your share? Broadly speaking, there are three options:

a Gift to surviving spouse
The effect of a gift of this sort is to ensure that the surviving spouse owns the family home outright and has complete control over it and its proceeds of sale.

b Gift to adult children

The effect of such a gift is that the family home will be owned jointly by the surviving spouse and their children as tenants in common. This arrangement, which guarantees the surviving spouse a right to occupy the family home, will only work satisfactorily in practice provided that there is a harmonious relationship between the two generations. If there is not, do not use this route.

In terms of saving IHT, joint ownership of the family home by the surviving spouse and their children as tenants in common may be effective in reducing the size of the taxable estate on second death. We recommend that you do not go along this route without obtaining full legal advice.

c Gifts outside of the family

The effect of a gift like this would be to make the family home owned jointly by the surviving spouse and someone outside the immediate family. This route should not be followed without obtaining full legal advice.

7.3 Business property relief

The owner of business property can sometimes dispose of their interest in that property without paying any IHT at all or paying it at a reduced rate.

In order to qualify for this relief, two conditions must be complied with:

- normally, the transferor must have owned the business property for at least two years before their death; and
- the business property must fall within the prescribed categories.

If you think that part of the estate of the deceased may qualify for business property relief, you should obtain suitable professional advice.

7.4 Agricultural property relief

The owner of agricultural property can sometimes dispose of their property without paying any IHT at all or paying at a reduced rate.

In order to qualify for this relief, two conditions must be complied with:

- The transferor's interest must be in 'agricultural property'. Broadly speaking, this means farmland or farm buildings used with that land.
- The transferor must have either:

  occupied the property for agricultural purposes for at least two years before their death, or

  owned the property at least seven years before their death, during which period it was occupied by someone for agricultural purposes.

The transfer of shares in a farming company may also qualify for relief.

Entitlement to agricultural property relief is not straightforward so if you think a disposal may qualify you should obtain suitable professional advice.

7.5 Summary

We have covered a lot of ground in this chapter. The key issues to bear in mind when undertaking an estate planning exercise are:

- Put people's interests before tax saving considerations. This is particularly important in relation to the family home which, as we have seen, is not usually suitable for a tax planning exercise.
- IHT can be saved by making full use of all the exemptions and reliefs available to you in your particular circumstances.
- Gifts to children usually involve the creation of a trust.
- In the case of gifts of residue in particular, always choose an alternative recipient of the gift in case the primary beneficiary dies before you do.

08

how to make
your will legal

In this chapter you will learn:
- the rule about written wills
- exceptions to this rule
- who can witness a will
- rules about signing the will.

If you have followed all the instructions and examples in the previous chapters then you should have a will ready to be signed and witnessed. This chapter now deals with all the formal requirements of the law that are needed to make sure that your will is legally valid.

8.1 The need for the will to be in writing

As already stated in Chapter 04 the most important point is that a will must be written down. This includes typed (or word-processed) as well as hand-written wills. If you use a computer, the will must be printed out; merely having it on disk is not enough. Video wills are not legally enforceable.

8.1.1 Exceptions

Those in the forces on active service and sailors at sea can make a verbal will. The reasoning behind this is that in the middle of a battle or when a ship is sinking it is not practicable to write down a formal will. There must be two witnesses who hear what is said. This rule is still relevant today as illustrated by a real case decided in 1981.

Case study

Jones was a soldier serving in Northern Ireland, who was shot. He was taken to hospital and on the way there he said in front of officers 'If I don't make it, make sure that Anne gets all my stuff.' Anne was his fiancée and they were due to be married the next week. Jones died and there was then a dispute as to whether his statement in front of two witnesses was a valid will. If it was not, then his parents would inherit as his next of kin. The court decided that there was a valid will and that Anne should inherit all his possessions.

8.2 Witnesses to the will

There must be **two** witnesses to a will. The important points to note are:

1 Witnesses must be 'competent'. This means that they must be able:

- to see the testator sign – for this reason a blind person cannot be a witness
- to understand that they are witnessing a signature – so they must be mentally capable of doing this.

  Note: there is no set lower age limit for witnesses, but it is better not to ask anyone under 18 to be a witness, just to make sure that there is no query.

2 A witness (or the spouse of a witness) **cannot** benefit from the will; if any money is left to a witness (or their spouse), they will not be able to receive it, but the rest of the will is valid. For this reason do not let anyone who has been left anything in the will be a witness.

3 An executor should not witness the will, because it will prevent him or her from reclaiming costs of dealing with the estate.

4 Exceptions to the need for witnesses: if those in the forces on active service or sailors at sea make a written will, they do not need to have it witnessed.

8.3 Signing the will

It is very important that a will is correctly signed, both by the person making the will and the witnesses. So read the following carefully:

- **Date** – put the date of the day on which the will is signed; the date should be put in before the witnesses sign.

  Note: Strictly speaking it is not legally necessary to put the date on the will, but it will lead to problems if the date is not on it. For example, it will be impossible to tell which is the later of two wills.

- **Testator's signature** – this should be done in the presence of both witnesses. This means that both witness must be there together when the testator signs and they must be able to see him sign.

  Alternatively the testator can sign in private and then acknowledge the signature as his to the witnesses, by saying something like 'this is my signature'. This acknowledgement must be in the joint presence of the witnesses, that is the two witnesses must be there together.

  If the testator is illiterate and does not know how to write, then he can make a mark, such as a cross, instead of a signature.

- **Where should the testator sign?** – it is best to sign immediately after the last line of the will.

  Signing at the end is not a strict legal requirement. In fact, the law recognizes a will as valid so long as the testator has signed it somewhere with the intention of signing the document as his will. The reason for suggesting that the signature should be at the end means that there is no confusion about it and it also makes sure that nothing can be added to the will.

- **Witnesses' signatures** – each witness must sign the will. This must be done in the presence of the testator. It is not necessary for each witness to see the other witness sign, but it is more sensible to make sure that they do stay while all the signatures are completed.

- **Where should the witnesses sign?** – the best place is immediately below the testator's signature at the end of the will.

- **Information about the witnesses** – it is not necessary for witnesses to do anything except sign, but it is recommended that they should add their address after their signature. This helps to identify the witnesses, so that if there is any doubt about the validity of the will after the testator dies, the witnesses can be contacted (assuming they are still alive!).

- **Attestation clause** – this is a statement that the witnesses were present together and that they both saw the testator sign. The suggested wording for this is:

  'Signed by the testator (testatrix) in our joint presence and then by us together in his (hers)'

  If this is not included, then, after the testator's death in order to have the will recognized as genuine, it will be necessary to contact one of the witnesses and get them to make a sworn statement about what happened when the will was signed. If the testator dies several years after the will was made, it may not be possible to trace the witnesses or the witnesses themselves might have died. So avoid these potential problems by making sure that an attestation clause is included just above or alongside the witnesses' signatures.

The end of a will should look something like this:

Example

Testator's signature...

Date...

Signed by the testator in our joint presence and then by us together in his

Witness signature...

of ....(address)

Witness signature...

of ....(address)

8.4 What to do if the testator wants to make a will but is incapable of signing

There are people who are physically disabled and cannot sign, but still wish to make a will. In these situations, provided that the person is mentally capable of making a will, the law allows someone else to sign the will on their behalf and at their direction. This person should sign their own name and make it clear that it is on behalf of the testator. This person can also be one of the witnesses, but it is better that it is a different person.

The testator and the person who signs on his behalf must be present together **and** the witnesses must be present together. The witnesses must hear the testator give his instructions that the will be signed by the other person and they must be able to see that other person sign. The witnesses then sign in the testator's presence.

The attestation clause needs to be different. The best form of words would be:

'Signed by .... (name) on the direction of the testator and in the testator's presence and in our joint presence and then by us together in the presence of the testator.'

09

how to change your will

In this chapter you will learn:
- how to make alterations to the original will
- how to make a codicil
- how to make a new will
- about revoking (canceling) your original will.

Once you have made a will, something may happen that makes you want to change it. It may be that one of the beneficiaries dies, or you may want to add in another gift. This chapter tells you how to go about changing your will.

9.1 Making alterations to the original will

The first point to note is that it is not a good idea to alter the original will. If you cross out parts of your original will or write extra bits in, the law will only recognize such changes if they are signed by the testator and witnesses. If this is not done then, even if a part is crossed out, the courts ignore the fact that it has been crossed out and take that part as still being in the will. In the same way additions are ignored. The strictness of this rule can be seen from a case that was decided in 1990. In this case the testator had made some changes to the original will and then written at the bottom of the will 'Alterations to will dated 14.12.84. Witnessed.' Two witnesses then signed below this. Despite this clear statement, the court would still not accept the alterations as changing the original will, since the actual alterations were not signed or initialled by the testator or the witnesses.

9.1.1 Effect of unsigned changes

If there is an unsigned change to a will, then if the original words are readable, the courts will only take notice of the original words. If the original words are no longer readable, then legally the crossed out words are treated as a blank space.

Example 1

> 5,000

I leave £2,000 to my nephew, James John Allen.

The change has not been signed and witnessed, so the change will be ignored. The original amount of £2,000 is still readable so that is the amount that counts. James John Allen will only be allowed to claim £2,000 under the will.

Example 2

5,000

I leave £■■ ■■ to my nephew, David Daniel Allen.

In this example it is not possible to read what was written originally just by looking at the will. Since there is another amount written in over the top, the law allows other methods (than just looking at the paper) to try and find out the original amount. These other methods can include using infra-red rays. If the original amount can be discovered, that is the amount David Daniel Allen will get. If the original amount cannot be read by any means, then David Daniel Allen will get nothing.

Example 3

I leave £■■ ■■ to my nephew, Patrick Paul Allen.

In this example, although the original is crossed out, there is nothing written in its place. Therefore the law assumes that the testator meant to cross out the whole gift to Patrick Paul Allen. As a result Patrick Paul Allen gets nothing.

9.1.2 Summary

So the best advice is do NOT make alterations on the actual will. If you do, you must be very careful to sign the will by the place of the alteration in the presence of two witnesses and then get the witnesses to sign at the same place. These signatures can be in the margin alongside the point where the change is. If there is more than one change then the testator and witnesses must sign each change. All the rules about witnessing wills (set out in Chapter 08) still apply, so check these.

9.2 Making a codicil

The best way to make minor changes to a will is to make a codicil. A codicil is a separate document made after the original will that adds to or alters that original will. This is a suitable way of dealing with small changes; for example, increasing the amount you want to leave your nephew. It can also be used to add a new person into the will; for example, if you now want to leave £1,000 to a friend whom you had not left anything to in the original will. But note that if you want to make several changes, then the best way is to make a completely new will.

9.2.1 How to make a codicil

The wording of a codicil will depend on the exact changes you want to make. If you only want to make one change the wording can be short and simple. The codicil should start by stating that it is made as an addition to your will. Then write down the gift that you want to leave, making sure that the words used are clear and that the person who is being left the gift is identified.

The same rules for making a will apply to codicils. This means that a codicil must be:

* in writing
* signed or acknowledged by the testator in the presence of two witnesses
* signed by the witnesses in the presence of the testator.

Example 1

In this example the testator had not left anything in his original will to his nephew, James John Allen.

1 This codicil is made by me, Henry Allen, as an addition to my will dated 19 February 1998.

2 I give £5,000 to my nephew, James John Allen.

3 In all other respects I confirm my will.

Testator's signature...

Date..

Signed by the testator in our joint presence and then by us together in his

Witness signature...

of ....(address)

Witness signature...

of ....(address)

Example 2

In this example the testator had left £2,000 to his nephew in his will, but now wants to increase that amount.

1 This codicil is made by me, Henry Allen, as an addition to my will dated 19 February 1998.

2 I revoke the gift in that will of £2,000 to my nephew, James John Allen.

3 I now give £5,000 to my nephew, James John Allen.

4 In all other respects I confirm my will.

Testator's signature...

Date..

Signed by the testator in our joint presence and then by us together in his

Witness signature...

of ....(address)

Witness signature...

of ....(address)

If you want to make a large number of changes then it is better to make a new will and revoke (cancel) your old will.

9.3 Making a new will

The rules for making a new will are the same as for making your first will. These rules are explained in Chapters 02 to 08 and you should read these chapters before making a new will.

The extra point to note is that you must make it clear in your new will that the old one is cancelled. This is why it is suggested that all wills should start with the words 'I revoke all previous wills and codicils'.

If you do not make it clear that your new will cancels all previous wills, then only the parts of the old will that conflict with the new will are cancelled. Other parts may still be counted. This is explained by the following example.

The gift of your car to your son is cancelled as that conflicts with the gift to your brother in the second will. The gift of £5,000 to your daughter is cancelled as it is replaced by £10,000. Your wife will inherit the house under your second

Example

In your first will, you left your car to your son, £5,000 to your daughter and everything else to your wife. In your second will you left your car to your brother, £10,000 to your daughter and your house to your wife.

will, but the second will does not say what should happen to any other possessions (e.g. the furniture) or money that you have. So, if the old will still existed, the courts would look back to it and say that your wife inherits everything else (i.e. everything that is not specifically mentioned in your second will).

Note that there are other ways of revoking your original will, even if you do not make a new one and these are explained next.

9.4 Revoking your original will

There are two main ways that you can revoke your original will without making a new one. These are:

• *Making a formal declaration that the will is revoked.* This can be done without making another will. The declaration must be signed and witnessed in the same way as a will. It can be very short, for example:

I, Henry Allen revoke all my previous wills

Then it must be signed and witnessed as for a will, including an attestation clause.

• *Deliberately destroying the will.* If a testator intentionally destroys his will or orders someone else to destroy it in his presence, then that will is revoked. The will can be destroyed by any means, as the Wills Act 1837 says that a will is revoked by 'burning, tearing or otherwise destroying' it.

9.4.1 Problems

The main problem with both these methods of revoking a will is that there is nothing put in its place and so the person is considered as dying intestate, that is without any will. The laws of intestacy have to be applied to decide who inherits (see Chapter 13).

9.4.2 Destruction that does not revoke the will

If the destruction is accidental, perhaps in a house fire, then, provided there is evidence of what the will said (possibly from a copy kept in a bank or a solicitor's office), the will is still valid and can be used to decide who inherits.

If someone else destroys the will without orders from the testator and/or not in the presence of the testator, then again the will is still valid and, if there evidence of what was in it, this is used to decide who inherits.

9.4.3 Revocation through marriage or divorce

You should note that both getting married and getting divorced can revoke or partly revoke any will made before these events. These points are considered in the next chapter.

9.5 Summary

So the best advice is:

- Do not make changes on the actual will.
- Use a codicil for small changes.
- Make a new will for major changes.

10

change of circumstances

In this chapter you will learn:
- about the effect of getting married on an existing will
- about the effect of getting divorced on an exisiting will.

10.1 The effect of marriage on a will

If you make a will and later get married, that will is revoked (that is considered by law to be cancelled) by that marriage. The reason is that the law assumes that your wishes will change as you now have a spouse to consider. If you do not make another will then you die intestate and the rules as to who inherits on an intestacy will apply. These rules are set out in Chapter 13.

There are two main problems to this situation and these depend on the value of the estate that you leave and whether you have children or parents still alive or brothers and sisters. The first problem is that if you have more than £125,000 your spouse may not get all your estate. This could create the situation of your spouse having to sell the family home after your death in order to pay some of the estate over to family members.

The second problem is that if you leave less than £125,000, then any children of a former marriage (or of your present marriage) will not inherit anything as, under the rules of intestacy, it will all go to your spouse.

To avoid the awkwardness of having to sign a new will immediately after you get married (and the worst scenario is that you could be killed in an accident as you leave the church or the registry office), you can make a will in contemplation of marriage.

10.1.1 A will in contemplation of marriage

This is a will made before your marriage, when you intend getting married, and is not intended to be revoked by the marriage. You cannot make a will like this in a general way – that is without a particular person in mind. The safest way to make sure that the will is not revoked by your marriage is to use specific words in the start of the will saying that it is made knowing that you are going to get married to a particular person and that the will is made in contemplation of that marriage.

Example

This will is made by me, Adam Hall, in contemplation of my marriage to Eve Green.

However, the law is not as strict as it used to be and provided it is clear from the will that it is made in contemplation of marriage, specific words at the start of the will are not required. For example, one of the clauses may read: 'I give the residue of my estate to Eve Green, whom I am going to marry.' But if you want to be sure the will is effective then it is safer to use the words in the example at the start of the will.

10.1.2 What happens if the marriage does not take place?

If the planned marriage does not take place, the will is not revoked, unless (and until) it is revoked in some other way. A way to make sure that the will is only effective if you marry the named person is to put extra words in saying that the will ceases to be of effect if the marriage to that person does not happen within six months. This means that the will is automatically revoked after the period of six months.

If you do not make the will conditional upon your marriage, then it can still be revoked by any of the methods discussed in Chapter 09. Also, it is important to realize that it will be revoked if you get married to someone other than the person indicated in the will.

10.2 The effect of divorce on a will

A divorce has the effect of cutting out your ex-spouse from your will. All the rest of the will remains valid. This is because, not surprisingly, the law assumes that as you are divorced, you will not want your former partner to inherit any of your property.

10.2.1 What happens to property left to a former spouse?

The situation is that any property left to a spouse does not go to that spouse after divorce. Instead the property goes to whoever would have inherited it had the spouse died at the date of the divorce. The only time that this rule will not be applied is if the testator has specifically said in the will that divorce does not affect it.

Note: This does not prevent the ex-spouse from making a claim for financial provision to be made for them from the testator's estate. The law on this is considered in Chapter 14.

10.2.2 What if the former spouse was appointed executor or trustee?

The law states that any provision appointing a former spouse as executor or trustee will take effect as if the former spouse had died before the testator. So, if in the will there are three trustees appointed, one of whom is the former spouse, then the other two trustees will be appointed. However, if there was a statement in the will that if one of the trustees died before the testator, then another person was to be a trustee, this would take effect. That is, the other person will become a trustee instead of the former spouse, even though the former spouse is still alive.

10.2.3 What if the former spouse was appointed as guardian to any children of the family?

Any appointment by the testator of the former spouse as guardian is revoked, unless the will specifically states that divorce does not change the appointment.

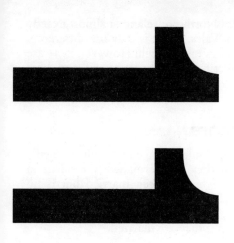

11

making a will in Northern Ireland

In this chapter you will learn:
- the different rules for making a will in Northern Ireland.

The law on making a will in Northern Ireland is almost exactly the same as in England and Wales. There is only one difference. This is that married minors can make a will. However, there are some differences in who inherits when there is no will and these are set out in Chapter 15.

11.1 Married minors

Anyone over the age of 16 but under the age of 18 who is legally married can make a will if they are permanently resident in Northern Ireland. A minor who has been married but is no longer married can also make a will. These rules have applied since 1 January 1995. In England and Wales it is not possible for a minor to make a will, even if they are married.

For the rest of the rules relating to making wills you should read Chapters 02 to 10.

making a will in Scotland

In this chapter you will learn:

- who can make a will in Scotland
- how to word your will
- how to sign the will and get it witnessed
- the legal rights of your spouse and children that you cannot change by a will
- about survival of beneficiaries
- how to revoke a will.

The law in Scotland is completely different to that of England and Wales, so if you are domiciled in Scotland (that means that your permanent home is there), then this is the chapter you need to read before making your will.

Other matters under Scottish law are dealt with in later chapters. Who inherits where there is no will is in Chapter 16 and distributing an estate after a death is in Chapter 23.

12.1 Who can make a will?

Anyone from the age of 12 upwards can make a will in Scotland, provided Scotland is their permanent home. There is no upper age limit. The only other rule is that the testator must be of sound mind. People with a physical disability can make a will. Blind people may sign their own wills but, if they prefer, there is a special procedure which they can use instead. This procedure can also be used by anyone who is incapable of writing and it is explained on page 61.

12.2 Wording your will

The main point is to keep the will as simple and clear as possible. Make sure that you state your own name and address clearly at the start of the will. Describe the property you are leaving, so that it can be easily identified. Give full details of the person to whom you are leaving property, so that there is no dispute over who it is.

You should also realize that, if you are married or have children or grandchildren, you cannot disinherit your spouse or your descendants. They are able to claim 'legal rights' in your estate. These are explained later in this chapter.

12.3 Signing and witnessing the will

The testator must sign and date the will at the end. In addition, if there is more than one page, each of the earlier pages must be signed at the bottom of the page.

A blind person or anyone who is unable to write (e.g. because they are paralyzed or because they are illiterate) can ask a solicitor, advocate, sheriff clerk or justice of the peace to read the will out to them and then, instead of the person signing, they ask the official to sign the will for them. They must sign at the end of each page of the will and also at the very end of the will. The signature of the official must be witnessed by one witness.

If you are concerned with a will made before 1 August 1995, the rules were different. A will that had been signed by the testator but had not been witnessed was valid. However, this was so only if the whole will was written in the testator's handwriting. This was known as a holograph will. Or, if the will was typed, the testator had to write above his signature at the end of the typed will the words 'adopted as holograph'.

12.3.1 Witnessing the will

Only one witness is needed and any person aged 16 or over can be a witness. The witness must either see the testator sign the will or, if the testator has already signed the will, the testator must acknowledge the signature to the witness. This means the testator must show the signature to the witness and say that the signature is his.

The witness must then sign at the end of the will and their name and address must be included on the will. This is usually done in what is called the testing clause. The testing clause should also have the date of the signing of the will in it.

Example of a testing clause

In witness whereof I have signed this will on this page[1] at Inverness on 16 August 2003 before the witness, Ian Hamilton, computer analyst, of 15 Town Crescent Inverness.

Witness's signature.............................

....Testator's signature

[1] This assumes the will was only one page long; if it is longer then extra words must be added to refer to all the pages. For example a three-page will would need the words 'on this page and the previous two pages'.

The witness does not have to know what is in the will. A major difference between English law and Scottish law is that witnesses can inherit from the will. A witness in Scotland does not lose any legacy just because they have witnessed the will.

However, it is better not to ask a beneficiary to be a witness as it is a factor which can be used to challenge the will.

If you are concerned with a will that was made before 1 August 1995, it is necessary to realize that before that date a will needed two witnesses, except where it was a holograph will.

12.4 Legal rights of spouse and descendants

In Scotland it is not possible to make a will that completely disinherits your spouse or your descendants. Descendants means your children/grandchildren and so on. The law gives them what are known as 'legal rights' to part of your property.

1 If you have a spouse but **no** descendants (children or grandchildren, great-grandchildren, etc.), your spouse has the legal right to half of your moveable property. If you have left your spouse less than this the spouse can claim their 'legal rights' instead of what is in the will. But they cannot claim both, they must choose which they want; their 'legal rights' or the property left to them in the will. It is also necessary to realize that the legal rights are only in moveable property, that is furniture, car, jewellery, money and so on. A spouse does not get legal rights in a house or other interest in land.

2 If you leave a spouse **and** descendants, then the spouse only has legal rights in one third of the moveable property; the descendants are also entitled to one third. This will be equally divided between any children and will only go to grandchildren, etc., if the child who was their parent has already died.

3 If your spouse has already died but you leave descendants, then those descendants are entitled to one half of the moveable property. Again this half will be divided between the children and only go on down to subsequent generations if a child of the testator had died before the testator.

This sounds quite complicated so a flow chart (see Figure 12.1) setting out the order in which legal rights are given is shown on the following page.

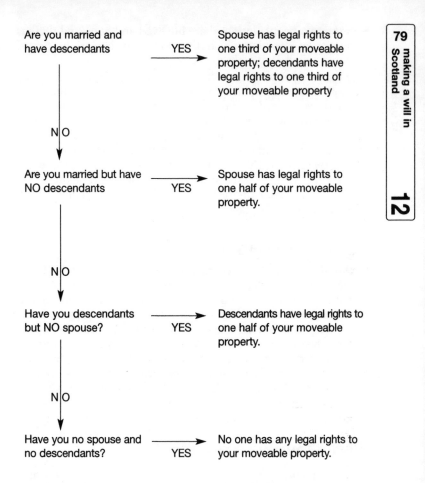

figure 12.1 Scottish legal rights of spouse and descendants

12.5 Survival of beneficiaries

Another way in which Scottish law differs from English law is on the question of what happens if the testator and a beneficiary die in the same accident. Does that beneficiary inherit under the will? The basic points on this are:

- If it can be shown that a beneficiary survived by even an instant, then that beneficiary inherits anything left to them in the will.

- If the two people involved are husband and wife, and there is no way of knowing which died first, then they are presumed to have died at exactly the same moment.
- If the two people are **not** husband and wife, and if there is no way of deciding which of the two died first, then the older person is deemed to have died before the younger one. So, if the testator was the older of the two, the beneficiary inherits what was left to them in the will. This could happen if, for example the testator had left a legacy to his younger sister, and the two of them had then been killed in the same car crash; because the sister was younger she would be presumed to have survived the testator and she (or rather her estate) would inherit the legacy.

12.5.1 Beneficiary dies before testator

In this situation, if the beneficiary was a child, grandchild, etc. of the testator or a nephew or niece or a descendant of a nephew or niece, then any descendants of the beneficiary would inherit the legacy, unless the will states that this is not to happen. If the beneficiary was not in one of these categories then the legacy lapses. This means that if it was a legacy of specific property it becomes part of the residue of the estate. If the legacy was the residue or a share of the residue, then the legacy becomes intestate estate and goes to whoever inherits if there is no will (see Chapter 16).

12.6 Revoking a will

As in England, a will is revoked (cancelled) by the testator making a later will revoking the earlier one. A will can also be revoked by destroying it. The testator does not have to destroy it personally, nor do they have to be present when the will is destroyed, they can instruct someone else to do it for them. For example a testator, whose will was at a solicitor's office, could write to that solicitor asking for the will to be destroyed. The solicitor could then shred the will at the office. This would revoke the will.

12.6.1 Effect of marriage on a will

In Scotland a person's will is not automatically revoked when they marry. However, the spouse will get the legal rights described earlier in this chapter. If you want your spouse to have more than their legal rights, it is sensible to make a new will when you get married, leaving anything you want to your spouse.

12.6.2 Effect of divorce on a will

If you get divorced after making a will in which you left property to your ex-spouse, then that gift is not automatically cancelled. However, you can arrange for this to happen by the wording of the will, for example by saying 'I leave £20,000 to my wife on condition that we are still married at the time of my death.'

part two

intestacy

13

who inherits if there is no will?

In this chapter you will learn:
- what is meant by intestate and intestacy
- the rules of intestacy where there is a surviving spouse
- the rules of intestacy where there is no surviving spouse.

There is only one key point covered in this chapter and that is who will inherit your property if you die without a valid will.

13.1 What is meant by intestate and intestacy?

Dying without making a will is legally called dying intestate. An intestacy is the situation of there being no will. The rules of intestacy decide who will inherit your property.

You will be considered to have died intestate if:

- you never made a will or
- you made a will but it was revoked and not replaced with another will.

You will be considered to have died *partially intestate* if:

- the will you made does not cover all your property or
- one (or more) of the beneficiaries in your will has died before you and the will did not say what should happen to the property left to the beneficiary in this situation.

In these cases the rules of intestacy apply to that part of the property.

Where someone has died intestate and left a large estate, there is the possibility of making a Deed of Variation after the death so as to avoid tax. However, such a Deed can only be made if all the beneficiaries who would inherit under the intestacy agree to it. If you think you may be in this situation then it is important to seek legal advice quickly.

13.1.1 Rules of intestacy

Intestacy rules basically follow the pattern that the spouse and/or the nearest blood relative(s) inherit. The exact order of who inherits is set down by law. The most important factor is whether the person who has died was married at the time of their death or not, as there are different rules for those who die married (that is leaving a surviving spouse) and those who die unmarried (that is without a surviving spouse).

13.2 Rules of intestacy where there is a surviving spouse

First it must be made clear that the term spouse only applies where the partners have been legally married. Even if partners have lived together for 40 or 50 years, the rules of inheritance do not recognize the survivor as the spouse. This means that such a partner will not inherit if there is no will. It is possible for a partner to claim that they are entitled to get something from the estate, but this claim will have to be made officially through the correct court proceedings. This is covered in the next chapter.

13.2.1 Spouse's rights to inherit

The spouse has the main rights to inherit but does not always inherit all the property. The first important rule is that in order to inherit the spouse must survive (that is live) after the death of their partner. By tradition, the survivorship period is usually 28 days.

The other factor is that if the deceased was survived by issue (this means children or grandchildren or great-grandchildren) or by parents or by brothers or sisters, then the spouse may not get all the estate. What the spouse will get depends on the value of the estate.

To sum up, the points that affect whether and how much the spouse will inherit are:

- Surviving the deceased (by 28 days).
- How much is the estate worth?
- Are there children (or grandchildren or great-grandchildren)?
- Are there parent(s) still alive?
- Are there brother(s) and/or sister(s) or their children?

So let's consider all these in turn.

a Spouse does not survive the other by 28 days

The estate will go to whoever would have inherited if there had not been a spouse. This is a fairly recent rule and applies where the deceased died on or after 1 January 1996.

If you are still trying to sort out the estate of someone who died before this date then the rule is that even if the spouse died the day after their husband or wife, that spouse would still inherit.

Where a husband and wife died in the same incident, for example a car crash, and it was not possible to say which one died first, then the rule used to be that it was assumed that the older of the two died first. This rule, which we looked at in section 5.2.3 of Chapter 05 (page 36) is known as the *commorientes* rule. It does not apply to spouses where the death is on or after 1 January 1996.

b The effect of the value of the estate

Where there is a child or children (or grandchildren, etc. of the deceased person) then the key value is £125,000. Where there are no children, but there are surviving parents or brothers/sisters of the deceased, the key value is £200,000. Where the estate is below these values the spouse inherits it all.

c There are children

First it is important to realize that 'child' and 'children' includes an adopted child or children, a child or children by a former marriage and any illegitimate child or children. Where a man dies, it also includes his children who have been conceived but not born at the date of his death. This idea is legally expressed by a French phrase *en ventre sa mere* which literally means in the mother's tummy! Provided the child is born alive it has the same rights of inheritance as any other child of the deceased. The word children does not, however, include stepchildren as they are not blood relatives.

d Children conceived by AIH or AID or IVF

AIH and AID are where a child is conceived by artificial insemination. For AIH the husband's semen is used; for AID semen from a donor is used. IVF refers to *in vitro* fertilization where an egg is taken from the woman and fertilized by sperm in a dish (*in vitro*). The sperm may be that of her husband or from a donor.

Where a couple are married any child conceived by artificial methods during the marriage is presumed to be a child of that marriage for the purposes of inheritance. It is only where the husband can prove that he did not consent to artificial insemination using donor semen that the courts can rule that such a child should not inherit. There is also an important exception that a title (e.g. Lord) cannot be passed on to a child where donor sperm is used.

When a woman who is not married has a child by AID then the donor of the sperm is treated as the father of the child.

e Dividing the estate between surviving spouse and children

Where there is a child or children, then if the estate is £125,000 or less the surviving spouse will inherit it all and the children get nothing. However, if the estate is more than £125,000 the spouse does not get it all. The spouse will inherit the first £125,000 plus all the personal belongings. The remainder of the estate is divided into two, and one half goes to the spouse, but only as a life interest. This means that the spouse will benefit from it during their life, and after their death it will go to the children. The other half is divided equally between the children. But the children must live until 18 years old or get married before that age for them to receive their inheritance. It is held on trust for them until then. If any of the children have already died but have left children of their own, then their share will be divided among these children.

This sounds complicated so let's use some examples to explain the rules more clearly.

Example 1

Anthony dies without making a will; his estate is worth £275,000. At the time of his death, his wife, Barbara, is still alive and she survives him by 28 days. They have three children; Carol, aged 24, who is married and has a child, Faith, aged 3; Dennis, aged 20; and Elsa, aged 17.

Barbara will inherit the first £125,000, plus the personal belongings, but the remaining £150,000 will be divided between her and the children so that she gets a life interest in half of it (£75,000) and the children share the other £75,000 as shown in Figure 13.1.

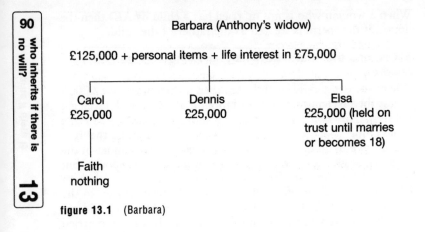

Barbara (Anthony's widow)

£125,000 + personal items + life interest in £75,000

Carol
£25,000

Dennis
£25,000

Elsa
£25,000 (held on
trust until marries
or becomes 18)

Faith
nothing

figure 13.1   (Barbara)

Example 2

Now let's take the same family but with the situation that Carol had died before her father. Her share would go to her daughter, Faith, but would have to be held on trust because Faith is only 3. This is shown below in Figure 13.2.

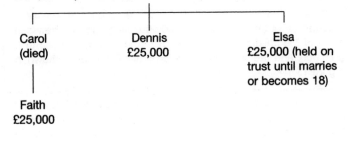

Barbara (Anthony's widow)

£125,000 + personal items + life interest in £75,000

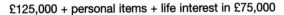

Carol
(died)

Dennis
£25,000

Elsa
£25,000 (held on
trust until marries
or becomes 18)

Faith
£25,000

figure 13.2   (Faith)

Example 3

Grant and his wife, Harriet, who have one child, Ian, aged 2, are involved in a car crash. Grant dies instantly, Harriet, who is eight months' pregnant, dies three days later after giving birth to a daughter, Jane. Harriet also has a son, Kevin, aged 10, by a former marriage. Grant's estate is worth £180,000.

As Harriet has not survived Grant by 28 days she will not inherit any of his estate. Kevin will not inherit as he is a stepson of Grant. But Jane will inherit, even though she had not been born when her father died. This is shown in Figure 13.3.

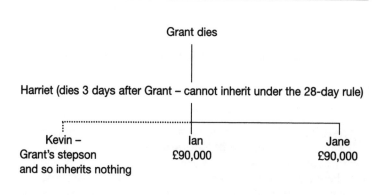

figure 13.3   (Grant)

f There are no children but the deceased's parent(s) are still alive

Where one or both parents are alive, it does not matter if the estate is £200,000 or less as the surviving spouse will inherit it all. The parents get nothing. However, if the estate is more than £200,000 the spouse does not get it all. The spouse will inherit the first £200,000 plus all the personal belongings. The remainder of the estate is divided into two, and one half goes to the spouse. The other half goes to the parent(s). So where only one is alive that parent gets all this half, but if both are still alive it is divided equally between them. Step-parents do not inherit as they are not blood relatives. An example is given opposite.

Example

Luke dies. He is survived by his wife, Maria, and by his mother, Nancy. Luke's estate is worth £260,000. His wife will get the first £200,000 plus all the personal belongings. The remaining £60,000 is divided into two, so £30,000 of this also goes to Maria and the other £30,000 to Nancy as shown in Figure 13.4.

Nancy (Luke's mother) £30,000

Luke

married to Maria £230,000 plus personal belongings

figure 13.4 (Nancy)

g There are no children nor are the deceased's parent(s) still alive, but there are brothers/sisters

For this rule brothers/sisters means full brothers/sisters and not half brothers/sisters. If the estate is £200,000 or less, the surviving spouse will inherit it all; the brothers/sisters get nothing. However, if the estate is more than £200,000 the spouse does not get it all. The spouse will inherit the first £200,000 plus all the personal belongings. The remainder of the estate is divided into two, and one half goes to the spouse. The other half is shared between the brothers/sisters. If any of the brothers/sisters have died before the deceased, then their share goes to their children.

This order of inheritance is shown in a flow chart (Figure 13.5).

13.2.2 Additional rights of the surviving spouse

Clearly there may be cases where, because some of the estate goes to the children or parents or brothers/sisters, the amount the spouse gets is not as much as the value of the home. This is particularly true in the south of England where property values are high. There are three ways in which a spouse can get more protection:

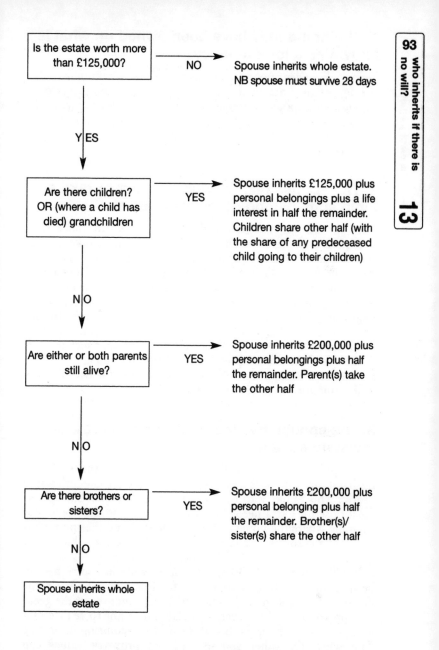

figure 13.5 who inherits where the deceased was married at time of death

1 The home may have been owned on what is known as a joint tenancy

Tenancy here does not have anything to do with renting a house. A joint tenancy means that the home becomes the property of the surviving spouse automatically. It does not form part of the estate in an intestacy. However, this will only happen if the two spouses arranged during their lifetime to own their home by a joint tenancy.

2 The spouse has the right to elect to take a lump sum instead of the life interest

They would get this when the estate is worth more than £125,000 and there are children. The decision to take a lump sum must be made within 12 months from the grant of representation to deal with the estate. The spouse must give notice in writing to the personal representatives of the deceased, or, if the spouse is the only personal representative, to the Senior Registrar of the Family Division of the High Court. In this situation it is probably better to seek legal advice, as the amount is calculated from set tables which take into account such matters as the age of the surviving spouse. If all the children are all of full age and mental capacity, an agreement can be made with them as to the amount the surviving spouse will get.

3 The spouse has the right to acquire the intestate's home

This applies to 'the dwelling house in which the surviving husband or wife was residing at the time of the intestate's death'. This is likely to be the matrimonial home. The spouse must raise the extra needed to reach the value of the home. For example where the home is worth £200,000 and the spouse has inherited the statutory £125,000 plus a life interest, which has a capitalized value of £25,000, then the spouse needs to raise £50,000 to acquire the home. One of the ways in which this can be done is by getting a mortgage for this amount. Again the decision to do this must be made within 12 months of the grant of representation. However, it is also important to realize that the value of the home is that at the date of acquiring it, not the date when the other spouse died. As property values can sometimes increase rapidly, it is essential that a surviving spouse makes this decision as quickly as possible.

13.3 Rules of intestacy where there is no surviving spouse

When a person dies and there is no surviving spouse, their nearest relative(s) will inherit. The order in which relatives rank for this purpose is:

1 **Children** – they will share the estate equally between them. If any child has died before the deceased, then that child's children inherit their parent's share. (Children has the same meaning as explained on page 88.)

2 **Parents** – if both parents are still alive then they share the estate equally, if only one parent is alive, that parent inherits the whole estate. Step-parents do not inherit.

3 **Brothers/sisters** – the estate is divided equally between them, so if there are two – each will get a half, if there are three – each will get a third, and so on. If any brother or sister has died, their children take their share.

4 **Half brothers/half sisters** – these only inherit if there are no full brothers or sisters. A half brother or sister is one who has one parent in common with the deceased. Stepbrothers/sisters do not inherit.

5 **Grandparents** – in equal shares if more than one is still alive.

6 **Aunts/uncles of the whole-blood** – this means aunts/uncles who had the same parents as either your mother or your father. They share equally. If any have died then their children take that share.

7 **Aunts/uncles of the half-blood** – this means aunts/uncles who had one parent in common with your mother or your father. In other words your parents' half brothers and sisters. They share equally. If any have died then their children take that share.

A flow chart setting out this order is shown in Figure 13.6.

Note that each category is considered in the order listed. It is only if there is no one in a particular category that the next category will be considered. Where one of those inheriting is under 18 years of age, then they will only inherit absolutely when they become 18 or marry under that age.

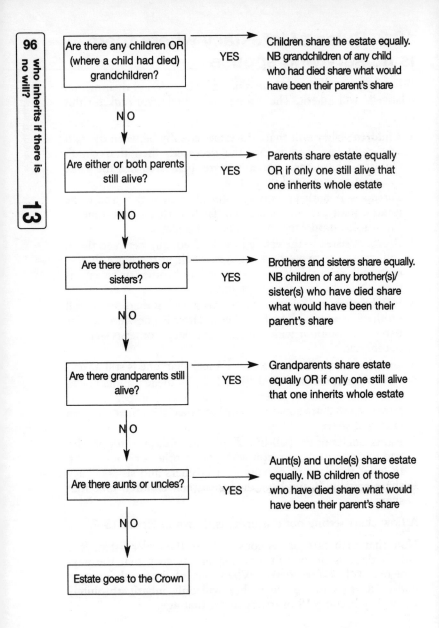

figure 13.6 who inherits where the deceased was NOT married at time of death

Example

Peter died without making a will. His estate is worth £300,000. His wife had died before him. Peter had three children, Robert who is illegitimate, and Sandra and Tim who were the children of his marriage. Tim was killed in a road accident seven years ago, leaving two children of his own, Una, aged 20, and Vince, aged 17. Sandra also has two children, William (21) and Yvonne (23).

As Tim has left children, the estate will be divided into three equal parts of £100,000 and Robert and Sandra will each inherit one part. The share that Tim would have got is divided between his children (£50,000 each). However, as Vince is under 18 his share is held on trust for him until he is 18. If he dies before then (and has not married) then his share will go to Una.

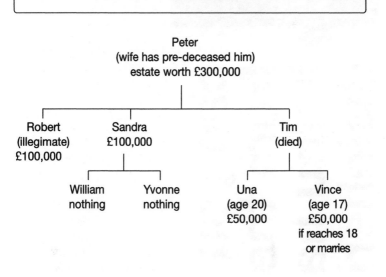

figure 13.7 (Peter)

13.3.1 No relatives

If there are no relatives in any of the above categories then the estate goes to the Crown (or the Duchy of Lancaster or the Duke of Cornwall).

14

can you claim from the estate if you have been disinherited?

In this chapter you will learn:
- who can apply for provision from an estate
- the time limit for making a claim
- how to make a claim
- what factors are considered on such a claim.

As you will have seen from the last chapter there are very rigid rules about who inherits if there is no will, so if you do not inherit where there is no will, can you do anything about it? Equally, what about the situation where there is a will but the testator did not leave you anything (or only a very small amount)? In both these cases the law recognizes that there may be a need to review the way in which an estate has been left and it is possible for changes to be made.

By the way, the law in Scotland is totally different as the concepts of 'legal rights' and 'prior rights' apply. These are explained in Chapters 12 and 16.

14.1 Who can apply for provision from an estate?

There are six categories of people who can apply to the courts for provision to be made for them from the estate of a deceased person. These categories are:

1 The spouse of the deceased.
2 A former spouse of the deceased who has not re-married.
3 A person who though not married to the deceased was, throughout the two years immediately before the person died, living with them as their spouse in the same household (a cohabitee).
4 A child of the deceased.
5 A person who, though not a child of the deceased, was treated as a child of the family by the deceased.
6 Any person who immediately before the death of the deceased was being maintained wholly or partly by the deceased.

These are reasonably self-explanatory, but there are some special points to note, so let's look at each of them in turn.

14.1.1 Spouse

This means anyone who was married to the deceased at the time he/she died. Even if husband and wife had separated, a spouse can make a claim for financial provision from the estate, provided they were still married. A claim can be made even if divorce proceedings had been started, again provided the decree absolute of divorce had not been granted.

14.1.2 Former spouse who has not re-married

Former spouse includes anyone whose marriage to the deceased has been dissolved or annulled. In other words there has been a divorce or the marriage has been declared to be invalid and the marriage annulled.

14.1.3 Cohabitee

This is a new category which has only been recognized since 1 January 1996. Before that date a cohabitee could not claim from their partner's estate, unless they could show that they were being maintained by the deceased (that is, they came within category 6 in the list). This created some very unfair situations where two people who had been living together for a long period of time, but had not made wills, did not inherit each other's property. The surviving cohabitee might even find that they had to move out of the home if it was in the dead partner's name. This is because under the laws of inheritance, the house would be inherited by the nearest relatives. This could even possibly be a relative whom the deceased had never met such as a nephew or niece. The law now recognizes that long-term partners who have lived as husband and wife should have some rights to claim from each others' estate.

In order to make a claim there are two points that the surviving cohabitee must be able to prove:

- that they had lived together as husband and wife for at least two years, and
- they were still living together immediately before the deceased died.

14.1.4 Child of the deceased

As well as children born to the deceased during a marriage this also includes:

- A child who has been conceived at the time its father dies, but has not yet been born; this is called legally a child *en ventre sa mere* – literally a child in its mother's tummy. When that child is born an application for financial provision may be made on its behalf.
- A child of a relationship outside marriage (illegitimate).
- A child born before its parents were married, but whose parents later did marry.

- An adopted child (but an adopted child cannot claim from the estate of its natural parents).

Although the word child is used, this does not mean that only young children can apply. An adult person who is a 'child' of the deceased can apply, although the courts are not very sympathetic to able-bodied adult children and will only make an order for financial provision in exceptional circumstances. The principles on which the courts decide applications are explained on pages 102–5.

14.1.5 Treated as a child of the family

This allows those who are not actually children of the deceased, but who were brought up as part of the family, to claim. This might includ stepchildren, or a nephew or niece. The important thing is that the deceased must have treated them as a child of the family.

14.1.6 Anyone else being maintained by the deceased

In order to come within this category it is not necessary to be a relative of the deceased or even to have lived in the deceased's household. The key points are:

- the person must not come within any of the previous five categories and
- immediately before the death, the person must have been maintained by the deceased.

This does not mean that the claimant has to have been completely maintained, but only that the deceased was making a substantial contribution towards their maintenance. This can be by money, for example paying rent or nursing home fees, or it can be by money's worth, such as the deceased allowing someone to live rent free in a flat belonging to the deceased.

There is no minimum period of how long the person must have been maintained. Even if the maintenance only started a month before the deceased died it is possible for the person to make a claim. However, the length of time is a factor that the court will take into consideration in deciding if, and for how much, an order for financial provision should be made.

14.2 The time limit for making a claim

A claim must normally be made to court within six months of personal representatives being given the right to deal with the estate. This is known as a grant of representation and means that if there is a will the claim must be made within six months of the grant of probate; if there is no will the claim must be made within six months of letters of administration being granted.

The time limit is quite short so it is important to act quickly. The court will sometimes allow a claim to be made after six months, but this is fairly rare and there must be special and substantial reasons for extending the time limit.

14.3 How to make a claim

The most sensible way is to seek legal advice; this is one of the times when you should go to a solicitor. But if you really want to do-it-yourself, then the first decision is which court to use. Claims can be dealt with by a County Court or by the High Court. Usually the best court is your nearest County Court. Cases in the County Court are usually dealt with more quickly and more cheaply than in the High Court. There are about 270 County Courts throughout England and Wales and the phone number and address of your local County Court will be in your telephone directory.

The County Court office will give you the correct form to fill in to make your claim. The County Court can deal with a claim for any amount of money, but there is the possibility that a claim started in the County Court will be transferred to the High Court if the amount is very large or the case involves complex points.

14.4 What factors are considered on such a claim?

14.4.1 Reasonable financial provision

The first point is that you must be able to show that the deceased's will (or intestacy) does not make 'reasonable financial provision' for you. Spouses are treated more favourably than other claimants. It is not possible to predict

103
the estate and
disinheritance

14

exactly what a court is likely to decide, but there are some guidelines that the court must consider when making its decision.

14.4.2 Common guidelines

There are general points that a judge will consider when deciding whether, and how much, the claimant should receive. These are:

- The financial resources and needs of the claimant now or in the foreseeable future.
- The size and nature of the estate; in general if the estate is very small the courts are not likely to give the claimant anything from that estate.
- Any obligations or responsibilities that the deceased had towards the claimant.
- Any obligations or responsibilities that the deceased had to those who inherit under the will or intestacy.
- Whether the claimant has any physical or mental disability.
- Whether anyone who inherits under the will or intestacy has a mental or physical disability.
- Any other matter including the conduct of the claimant; for example the fact that a daughter has spent years looking after her father will make the court more likely to award her provision from the estate, whereas the fact that a daughter or son of the deceased has not seen, or kept in contact with, their parent for years will make a court less likely to award them provision from the estate.

14.4.3 Spouses' claims

The standard used in deciding whether a spouse should be given provision from the estate is 'such financial provision as it would be reasonable in all the circumstances of the case, for a husband or wife to receive, whether or not that provision is required for his or her maintenance'. So the fact that the spouse already has money of their own does not stop them claiming from the estate, if the deceased left them nothing or very little.

The court will often start by considering what a spouse would have been likely to receive if the marriage had ended in divorce rather than by the death of one of the partners. The other special matters the court will consider are:

- the age of the claimant and how long the marriage lasted, and
- the contribution that the spouse made to the welfare of the family of the deceased, including looking after the home and caring for the family.

14.4.4 Claims by others

The standard used for others' claims is known as the 'maintenance standard'. In other words, the amount it would be reasonable in all the circumstances of the case for the claimant to receive for his maintenance. There are also some special points that will be considered for the different categories of claimant. These are:

a The former spouse

As with surviving spouses the court considers the age of the claimant and how long the marriage lasted; and the contribution that the spouse made to the welfare of the family of the deceased, including looking after the home and caring for the family. But, if there has already been a financial settlement when the divorce happened, then it is unlikely that the former spouse will be given any more.

If the divorce happened less than 12 months before the death, the court may decide to treat the former spouse as though they were the surviving spouse. This means that the court can apply the higher standard and award more than what is strictly necessary for their maintenance.

b A cohabitee

The court will only award what is necessary for their maintenance, but can take into consideration how long the relationship lasted, the age of the claimant, and the contribution made to the welfare of the family of the deceased. This is thought to provide a fair balance between recognizing the contribution made to the common household, but at the same time keeping a distinction between the claim of married and unmarried partners.

c A child of the deceased

An extra consideration here is the manner in which the child was being, or expected to be, educated or trained. This obviously applies to younger children, but it does not mean that grown-up children cannot claim; they can, but the courts will be less sympathetic to adult children who are capable of earning their own living.

d A child of the family

The same point above about education must be considered, but, since the child is not the deceased's child, the court will also consider:

- whether the deceased had assumed responsibility for the child's maintenance and, if so, the extent of this and the length of time it had gone on for
- whether in assuming responsibility for the child's maintenance, the deceased knew that the child was not his own; clearly if the deceased only looked after a child because he mistakenly thought it was his, then the obligations to that child are less
- the liability of any other person to maintain the child; clearly if there is someone else who should, and can, maintain the child (e.g. a natural parent) then the court is less likely to make an award from the estate.

e Any other person maintained by the deceased

The courts will look at the reason why the deceased was doing this and the length of time it had lasted.

Remember that the court is trying to be fair to all those who ought to have a share of the estate, and if the estate is small then it may not be possible to cater for all of them.

15

intestacy rules in Northern Ireland

In this chapter you will learn:
- the rules of intestacy in Northern Ireland where there is a surviving spouse
- the rules of intestacy in Northern Ireland where there is no surviving spouse.

When a person dies without making a will the rules for who should inherit in Northern Ireland are very similar to those in England and Wales, but there are some important differences. So in this chapter the different parts of the law are explained.

15.1 Rules of intestacy where there is a surviving spouse

The law on this is exactly the same as in England and Wales. This is already covered in detail on pages 87–9 in Chapter 13 so please read that section.

15.2 Rules of intestacy where there is no surviving spouse

When a person dies and there is no surviving spouse, their nearest relative(s) will inherit. In each case there must be no one in the earlier category for the next group to inherit. The order in which relatives rank for this purpose in Northern Ireland is:

15.2.1 Children

They will share the estate equally between them. If any child has died before the deceased, then that child's children inherit their parent's share. (Children has the same meaning as explained on page 88.)

15.2.2 Parents

If both parents are still alive then they share the estate equally. If only one parent is alive, that parent inherits the whole estate. Step-parents do not inherit.

15.2.3 Brothers/sisters

The estate is divided equally between any brothers and sisters, so if there are two, each will get a half, if there are three, each will get a third and so on. If any brother or sister has died, their children take their share. This category includes full brothers and sisters and half brothers and sisters. Full means that they have the same parents as the deceased. A half brother or sister is one who has one parent in common with the deceased. Step brothers/sisters do not inherit.

15.2.4 Grandparents

These are the next to inherit. If only one grandparent is alive they will inherit the whole estate. If more than one grandparent is still alive they will take it in equal shares.

15.2.5 Aunts/uncles

This category includes aunts/uncles who had the same parents as either your mother or your father and aunts/uncles who had one parent in common with your mother or your father. They share equally. If any have died then their children take that share.

15.2.6 Remoter relatives

If there is no one in any of the above categories then it is necessary to keep going back a generation, then coming down from a common ancestor to see if there are any relatives. So this would start by going back to great-grandparents and tracing their descendants. If there were none then you would have to go back to great-great-grandparents and trace their descendants and so on.

To help make this order clearer here is a flow chart setting it out (see Figure 15.1).

Remember that each category is considered in the order listed. It is only if there is no one in a particular category that the next category will be considered. Where one of those inheriting is under 18 years of age, then they will only inherit absolutely when they become 18 or marry under that age.

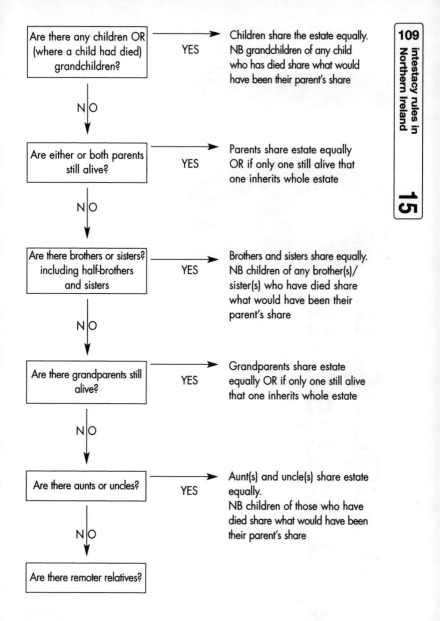

figure 15.1 who inherits where the deceased was NOT married at time of death (Northern Ireland)

16

intestacy rules in Scotland

In this chapter you will learn:
- the surviving spouse's prior rights in Scotland
- who inherits when there is a surviving spouse
- who inherits when there is no surviving spouse.

The law in Scotland on who inherits an estate where the deceased did not make a will is quite different to England and Wales.

16.1 Surviving spouse's prior rights

Under Scottish law the husband or wife of the deceased has the right to the first part of the value of the house, furnishings and an amount from the other moveable assets. Exactly what these rights are depends on whether there are children (or their descendants) or not. Prior rights are sufficiently large that the surviving spouse will often end up with the whole estate. In order to keep roughly in line with inflation, the amounts for prior rights are increased by the government about every five to seven years. In this book the figures are those set in 1999.

If the estate is larger than the amount of prior rights then the surviving spouse also has their legal rights in the remaining net moveable estate.

16.1.1 House

The surviving spouse has the right to the house up to the value of £130,000. If the house is worth only this amount or less then it means the surviving spouse inherits the house completely. If the house is worth more than £130,000 the surviving spouse will get £130,000 instead of it.

16.1.2 Furnishings

The legal words used are furniture and plenishings and the surviving spouse gets up to £22,000 in value of these. Furniture and plenishings includes garden effects, domestic animals, linen, glass, books, pictures and articles of household use. Carpets, furniture, television sets and washing machines are all examples of articles of household use. Items used for business are not included, nor are jewellery or money. The furniture and plenishings must be those in a home in which the deceased was ordinarily resident immediately before his or her death. Where the furnishings are worth more than £22,000, the surviving spouse may choose items to this value.

16.1.3 Other moveable assets

If there are children or their descendants, the surviving spouse also gets up to £35,000 from any other moveable assets. This includes items such as money in bank accounts and shares. If there are no children or descendants, but there are brothers or sisters (or their descendants) and/or the deceased's parent(s) are still alive then the surviving spouse gets up to £58,000.

16.1.4 Legal rights

Where an estate is large enough that there is still something left over after the surviving spouse has taken their prior rights, then the surviving spouse also has legal rights to part of the remainder. If there are children or their descendants, the surviving spouse has legal rights to one-third of the remaining net moveable estate. If there are no children or descendants, but there are brothers or sisters (or their descendants) or the deceased's parent(s) are still alive, then the surviving spouse gets one-half of the remaining net moveable estate.

From these rights you can see that the surviving spouse will get a substantial share of the estate, but that other people may be entitled to inherit part of the estate. So let's look at this next.

16.2 Who inherits when there is a surviving spouse

After the surviving spouse's prior rights and legal rights, the remainder of the estate goes to the deceased's closest relatives. If there are no close relatives, then the surviving spouse will inherit the whole estate. The close relatives who are entitled to a share are, first, children or their descendants, then brothers/sisters (or their descendants) and parents.

16.2.1 Children

If there are children then they share the remainder of the estate between them. Children include adopted children, but do not include stepchildren. Where a child of the deceased has died, but has left children of their own (these are grandchildren of the deceased), then the grandchildren share what would have gone to their parent. Similarly, if any of these grandchildren have already died but have left children (these are great-grandchildren of the deceased), then these great grandchildren share their parent's part of the estate. However, if all the first generation have died, then the next generation share equally.

As this sounds a little complicated let's look at some scenarios to show what will happen.

Example 1

Andrew has died. His wife died before him. His parents are also dead. Andrew had two children, Carol, who pre-deceased her father and Dennis, who is still alive. Carol had one child, Edward. Dennis has three children, Francis, Gina and Henry.

Andrew left property totalling £80,000 in value. As there were two children and one of them is still alive, this is divided in two. One half goes to Dennis. The other half goes to Carol's son, Edward. Francis, Gina and Henry get nothing because their father is alive.

So the family tree with the amount that each inherits looks like figure 16.1.

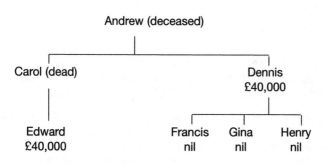

figure 16.1   inheritance rights of descendants

16.2.2 Brothers/sisters and parents

If there are no children or their descendants, then brothers/sisters (or their descendants) and parents inherit the remaining estate. If there are brothers/sisters (or their descendants) and parents then the remaining estate is divided into two. One half is divided between any brothers and sisters (if any have already died but have left descendants, then those descendants take their parents'

Example 2

Now what would happen if in the last example both Andrew's children have died before him? As there is no one of that generation left, the next generation will inherit equally. This means that the £80,000 that Andrew left is divided equally between all four grandchildren. So Edward, Francis, Gina and Henry each get £20,000.

The family tree with what each inherits now looks like this (see figure 16.2).

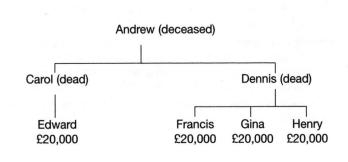

Figure 16.2 (Andrew)

share); the other half is divided between the parents. If only one parent is alive, that parent will take the complete half.

Brothers and sisters means those who have the same parents as the deceased. If there are no full brothers or sisters, then half brothers and sisters (that is those who have one parent in common with the deceased) will be entitled to inherit.

If there are no brothers or sisters or any descendants, then the parents share the whole of the remaining estate. If both parents have died then the whole of the remaining estate is divided between the brothers and sisters (or their descendants).

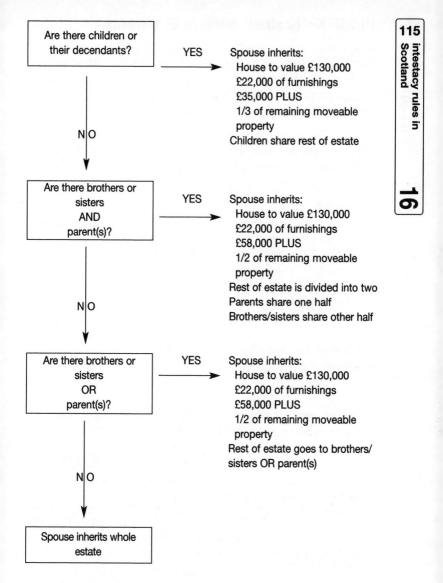

figure 16.3 who inherits on an intestacy under Scottish law where the deceased was married at time of death

16.2.3 No brothers/sisters or parents

Where there are no brothers or sisters nor any descendants and when both parents have died then the surviving spouse gets the whole of the estate.

To help make all this clearer there is a flow chart setting out this order of inheritance (see Figure 16.3).

To help you understand how the rules of prior rights and legal rights are applied, here are some worked examples. Remember these figures are based on those applying in 1999.

Example

Gordon has died leaving a house, furnishings, and savings. His wife Helen survives him. There are also two children, Angus and Ben. Gordon's parents are both dead.

PRIOR RIGHTS

	£	
Value of Gordon's house	180,000	
Less mortgage still owing	- 30,000	
Balance	150,000	
Spouse's prior rights	130,000	Helen gets this £130,000
Remaining	20,000	This is shared between Angus and Ben
Value of Gordon's furnishings	31,000	
Spouse's prior rights	22,000	Helen gets furnishings to the value of £22,000
Remaining	9,000	
Value of Gordon's other moveable assets	200,000	
Spouse's prior rights	35,000	Helen gets this £35,000
Remaining	165,000	

From the above we can see that Helen will get £110,000 from the house, £20,000 of furnishings plus £30,000 as her prior rights. In addition she will be entitled to legal rights in the remaining furnishings and moveable property. This is calculated next.

LEGAL RIGHTS

	£	
The remaining furnishings	9,000	+
Remaining moveable property	165,000	

	175,000	Helen gets one-third of this as her legal rights = £58,000

RIGHTS OF THE CHILDREN

The remaining two-thirds (£116,000) will be divided equally between Angus and Ben. They also share the remaining value of £20,000 from the house. So each gets a total of £68,000

16.3 Who inherits when there is no surviving spouse

When the deceased dies without leaving a surviving spouse, then the nearest blood relatives of the deceased inherit the estate. The order is as follows:

16.3.1 Children

The children share the estate equally between them. Children include adopted children, but do not include stepchildren. If a child has died, but has left children of their own (these are grandchildren of the deceased), then the grandchildren share what would have gone to their parent. Similarly, if any of these grandchildren have already died but have left children (these are great-grandchildren of the deceased), then these great-grandchildren share their parent's part of the estate. Again this will change if all of the first generation have died. In this case the next generation share equally. This same point is shown in Figure 16.2.

16.3.2 Brothers/sisters and parents

This is the next group to inherit if there are no children or descendants. If there are brother(s)/sister(s) **and** parent(s), then the estate is divided into two. One half is shared equally between the brothers and sisters or their descendants, the other half between the parents.

As in the previous section brothers and sisters means those who have the same parents as the deceased. If there are no full brothers or sisters, then half-brothers and sisters will be entitled to inherit.

If there are no brothers or sisters or any descendants, then the parents share the estate; if only one parent is still alive then that parent inherits the whole estate. If both parents have died then the estate is divided between the brothers and sisters or their descendants.

16.3.3 Uncles and aunts

The next people to inherit if there is no one in any of the previous groups are uncles and aunts or their descendants. Uncles and aunts means the brothers and sisters of the deceased's parents. If any of these have died but have children, then these share what would have been the uncle or aunt's share. If any of these have died but left their own children, then these will share what their parent would have received and so on down through the generations.

16.3.4 Grandparents

Next in the line of succession are grandparents. They share the estate between them or, if there is only one still alive, that one will inherit the whole estate.

16.3.5 Great aunts/uncles

Next are great aunts and uncles or their descendants. The same rule about children sharing their dead parent's share applies when considering descendants.

16.3.6 Remoter relatives

If there are no relatives in any of the above categories, then it is necessary to go back another generation at a time and look for their descendants to see if there are any surviving relatives.

16.3.7 The Crown

If there are no relatives that can be traced then the estate goes to the Crown. Officials will advertise for claimants, and if no relative claims the estate, the Crown may be prepared to make a gift from the estate to those who have a moral claim, such as a cohabitee.

To help make this order of inheritance clearer here is a flow chart showing it (see Figure 16.4 on page 120).

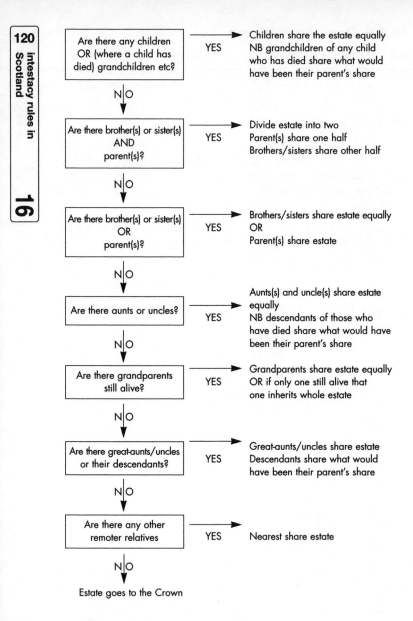

figure 16.4 who inherits under Scottish law where the deceased was NOT married at time of death

part

three

dealing with an estate

applying for probate

In this chapter you will learn:
- the steps that need to be taken by personal representatives after the death of a person who has made a valid will
- the duties of an executor
- an outline of the powers of an executor.

17.1 Steps following death

First questions

17.1.1 Who are the personal representatives?

The answer to this depends on:

- whether or not the deceased made a valid will
- whether or not the will contains a clause that legally appoints executors (this is known as effective appointment)
- whether or not those executors are able, ready and willing to carry out their duties.

If the deceased's will is valid and has an effective appointment of executors and the executors are prepared to act, then the executors are those people named in the will. However, there may be circumstances where one or more of the executors is either unwilling to act or unable to act (e.g. an executor may be too ill to act, or possibly one of the executors has died). No one has to act as an executor. If there are executors who are able and willing to act, then they can do so without the others.

Executor not able or willing to act

If you are named as executor in a will and are either unable to or do not want to act as executor, then you should sign a document known as a 'renunciation'. This is best prepared by a solicitor who can also advise you (and your co-executors, if any) how to proceed. If none of the named executors are willing to act then the people who would normally have been entitled to apply for letters of administration can apply for a grant of letters of administration.

Valid will but no effective appointment of executors

In this case those entitled to inherit under the will are entitled to apply for letters of administration (see Chapter 18).

Invalid will

If the deceased's will is not valid, then the executors named in that will cannot act as executors. Instead the nearest relative(s) are entitled to apply for letters of administration (see Chapter 18).

In this chapter, we look at the position of executors. In Chapter 18, we will look at the position of administrators.

17.1.2 What to do with the will

We have seen the authority of an executor to act as such comes from the will. It follows that the will should be found without delay so that the executors can be certain of their legal authority. Copies of the will should be made and given to each of the executors.

It is essential that the will is kept in a safe place, in the condition in which it was found. It must not be defaced or have anything attached to it – for example, a paper clip or staples.

17.1.3 Funeral arrangements

Executors should always be prepared to help with the funeral arrangements. In the case of a small estate, it is important that they should do this in order to keep an eye on the expenses.

17.1.4 The deceased's property

As we will see, executors are under a duty to take reasonable care of the deceased's property. Thus, one of the first steps to be taken is to ensure that the deceased's home, if it is unoccupied, is secure and any valuable items are in a safe place. You should also write to the deceased's bank, building society or mortgage lender to report the death.

17.1.5 The death certificate

You will need the death certificate issued by the Registrar of Deaths. Extra copies will be needed. The number you need depends on the size and extent of the estate. These can be obtained from the Registrar for a small fee.

17.2 Is a grant of probate necessary?

Broadly speaking, there are three situations in which executors can carry out their duties without needing to obtain a grant of probate.

17.2.1 Assets where no grant is needed to prove title

The Administration of Estates (Small Payments) Act 1965 allows some small payments to be made to the persons entitled to them without formal proof of title. The amount of a 'small payment' is reviewed by Parliament from time to time; it is currently £5,000 in England and Wales but there are plans to increase it. You cannot compel the payer to make the payment in the absence of probate. Payers that follow the Act include:

- Building societies and friendly societies
- The Premium Bonds office
- The National Savings Certificate office
- The National Savings Bank.

Executors are not usually required to prove their title to personal possessions and can usually sell items such as furniture without difficulty. But if the item concerned is valuable, probate may be needed.

The same applies to cash in the possession of the deceased (but not held in a bank or other account).

17.2.2 Assets not received by executors

There are two categories:

- Property held by the deceased as joint tenant: We have seen that property owned by two (or more) persons as joint tenants passes on death directly to the survivors. No grant is needed if the only assets of the deceased were held by him as a joint tenant.
- Nominated property: We have also seen that certain property can pass directly to nominees of the deceased's choice. No grant is therefore needed for nominated property to be passed on.

17.2.3 Property outside the estate

Broadly speaking, there are two categories here:

- Life insurance policies where the policy money was held in trust for someone else. Upon death, the insurer will pay the policy monies to the trustees of the policy, not to the executors of the deceased's estate.

- Pension benefits: As we saw in Chapter 03, pension benefits can be paid direct to the beneficiaries.

If you are an executor of a will of someone whose estate consists of one or more of the items listed above and nothing else, there is a strong probability that you will be able to wind up the estate without needing to obtain probate.

17.3 Preparing to obtain a grant of probate

We now look at the three steps that you need to take to apply for a grant of probate:

Step 1

As soon as you know that you are an executor and that a grant of probate will be necessary (or is likely to be necessary), contact the Personal Applications Department of the Probate Registry for the area in which you live and ask them to send you the relevant forms. A list of the Probate Registries will be found on pages 192–5. It is also available on the Internet at www.courtservice.gov.uk. A model letter of request to a Probate Registry is set out below. Alternatively you can visit www.courtservice.gov.uk for the forms you need.

The package you receive from the Probate Registry or download from the Internet will contain several forms. The probate application form (PA1) is straightforward. Currently, it comes with a leaflet 'How to Obtain Probate – a guide for the applicant without a solicitor' (PA2), which is very helpful. The Inland Revenue account (Form IHT 205) is straightforward and comes with a very helpful set of explanatory notes (Form IHT 206). We deal with the completion of the Inland Revenue account in Chapter 19.

49 Maradon Crescent
Cornford
7 May 2003
Loamshire
CD7 2BG

Personal Applications Department
Brighton District Probate Registry
William Street
Brighton
East Sussex
BN2 2LG

Dear Sirs

URSULA BENTHAM DECEASED FORMERLY OF 22 MAIN
STREET CORNFORD, LOAMSHIRE

I am an executor of the will of Ursula Bentham, who died a week
ago today, jointly with Mrs Bentham's sister, Veronica Strange.

Miss Strange and I wish to make a personal application for
probate of Mrs Bentham's will. Please send the necessary
application forms to me for completion.

Yours faithfully

Jeremy Watts

Step 2

When the relevant forms have been completed to the best of
your ability, you should:

- photocopy them and their accompanying enclosures
- photocopy the death certificate and the will of the deceased
- deliver the originals of the will, death certificate and relevant
  forms to the Probate Registry, personally or by guaranteed
  delivery post.

Normally, you will be invited to attend a meeting at the Probate
Registry within a few weeks of the despatch of this package.

Step 3

The purpose of the meeting at the Probate Registry is to enable the Registry officer to run through the completed forms and identify any area in which additional queries need to be made. All being well, everything will be in order and you will be asked to sign a document called the Executor's Oath. The law says that every application of probate must be accompanied by such an oath, which is really a means of assuring the courts that what you have said is true. Fortunately, the Probate Registry will prepare this document, which is technical and complex, so that we do not need to explain its details.

If any of the forms that you have submitted are not acceptable, the Probate Officer will explain what further information is needed and may be able to suggest where you might get it from. You may also be invited to another meeting.

Generally speaking, the grant of probate is issued about three weeks after your visit to the Probate Registry. A fee will be payable according to the gross value of the deceased's estate. These fees are reviewed from time to time so it is best to check what they are with the Probate Registry. If any inheritance tax is due, it must be paid before the grant of probate can be issued. We deal with this in Chapter 19.

17.4 The duties of an executor

The law says that the principal duty of an executor (and also an administrator), is to 'collect and get in' all the deceased's property and then to administer the estate according to law. Broadly speaking, there are three aspects to this.

17.4.1 Getting the assets in

This involves identifying the assets and collecting them together. This must be done within a reasonable time and if it is not, the beneficiaries of the deceased may be able to claim compensation for any loss they suffer as a result of the executor's unreasonable conduct. Assets include money owed to the estate such as a tax refund or a repayment of a loan.

17.4.2 Proving your title

In practice, you will probably find that the holders of the deceased's assets will not hand them over to you (unless the assets in question come within the categories mentioned on pages 126–7) until they have seen probate. You will need to show either the original grant or a court certified photocopy (called an 'office copy') of it. An ordinary photocopy will not usually be acceptable.

You will also usually need probate to prove your title to an asset that needs to be sold, for example, the home of an elderly person who divides the net proceeds of sale amongst his family.

17.4.3 What does the duty 'to administer' involve?

Broadly speaking, this means that you must make various payments stated in the deceased's will and then transfer what is left to the beneficiaries in accordance with the directions in the will. We deal with these aspects in greater detail in Chapter 20.

The probate courts can also make you prepare and deliver an inventory of the deceased's assets and a financial account of your dealings with them. In practice, this seldom happens unless there is a dispute or fraud.

The executor's year

Any personal representative, not just an executor, must carry out his duties within a reasonable time. What is reasonable is a question of fact in each case. A beneficiary normally has a right to insist upon his inheritance before the expiry of one year from the date of death – hence the expression 'the executor's year'.

17.5 Powers of executors

Executor's powers come from Acts of Parliament and sometimes the deceased's will. The statutory powers available to an executor (and to an administrator) include the trustees' powers, which we looked at briefly in Chapter 06. Our model forms of will, which you will find in Appendix 01, incorporate the statutory powers and include the most common current variations.

18

applying for letters of administration

In this chapter you will learn:
- the steps that need to be taken by personal representatives where there is no valid will
- the duties of an administrator
- an outline of the powers of an administrator.

18.1 Steps following death

18.1.1 First questions

We have seen that title to the deceased's property passes on death to their personal representatives. In the case of executors, their title stems from their appointment under the will. The function of a grant of probate, therefore, is simply to confirm the authority of the executors to the world at large.

Where there is no will at all or no valid will, the position of the deceased's personal representatives is significantly different. Their title to the deceased's assets does not exist until letters of administration have been granted. Consequently, their authority to deal with the deceased's estate between death and the issue of the grant is virtually non-existent. In this period, ownership of the deceased's assets is vested in the Public Trustee.

a Who are the personal representatives?

The identity of the personal representatives is determined by law and depends on whether the deceased made no will at all, a will that is invalid or an imperfect will.

b No will or an invalid will

There is a 'pecking order' of persons who may apply to be appointed. The order of appointment is broadly the same as the order of those who are entitled to a share of the deceased's estate under the Intestacy Rules. To qualify as a personal representative, the applicant must usually be entitled to inherit some or all of the deceased's estate under the intestacy rules.

c Imperfect will

If the deceased made a valid will that is imperfect in some way (for example, it contains no appointment of executors or the executors are unable or unwilling to act) the law will not allow a grant of probate to be issued. In these circumstances, the deceased's personal representatives are chosen from those who are entitled to inherit under the imperfect will.

d What sort of grant?

If the deceased made a valid will that is imperfect so that probate cannot be issued to an executor, the grant is called 'letters of administration with will annexed'. If the deceased made no will or one that is invalid, the grant is called 'letters of administration' or sometimes 'simple administration'. We use the expression 'simple administration' in this book to distinguish that grant from the other sort of letters of administration.

18.1.2 Practical considerations

The legal position of personal representatives of someone who has died without making a will or who has made an invalid or incomplete will is different to that of executors, as we have just seen. We can sum up an administrator's duty, pending the issue of the grant, by saying that it is to protect the deceased's estate from 'wrongful injury' during that period. Examples of wrongful injury, in this context, are matters such as trespass to land (for example, squatters) or allowing a tenant of the deceased's land to commit a breach of his obligations. If, therefore, you are a candidate to be an administrator, you should take care not to enter into any legally binding commitments until the grant has been issued to you. This should not prevent you from helping with funeral arrangements (if that is required), getting the Death Certificate and securing the deceased's property including any valuable items.

a Is a grant necessary?

Exactly the same considerations apply to the affairs of someone who has died without making a will or one that is invalid or incomplete as they do to a testator.

b Preparing to obtain a grant of letters of administration

The steps you need to take are the same as those set out on pages 127–9 in Chapter 17. If you are applying for a grant of simple administration, there will be no will to send to the Probate Registry.

18.2 The duties of an administrator

For practical purposes, these are the same as the duties of an executor. If there is no will or an invalid will, your duty will be to ensure that the deceased's residuary estate is disposed of in accordance with the intestacy rules. We dealt with this aspect in Chapter 13.

An administrator is under the same obligations to the probate courts as an executor to prepare and deliver an inventory and financial account. He must also carry out his duties within a reasonable time.

18.3 Powers of administrators

Broadly speaking, administrators have the same powers as executors, once letters of administration have been granted.

In this chapter you will learn:
- the duties of personal representatives in regard to taxation
- how to complete Inheritance Tax forms
- the effect of taxation on beneficiaries.

The administration of an estate usually involves three taxes:

- Income Tax
- Capital Gains Tax
- Inheritance Tax

to which personal representatives and/or beneficiaries may be liable.

In the first section, we look at the position of personal representatives, in the second we explain how personal representatives complete the necessary Inheritance Tax accounts and in the third we look at the position of beneficiaries.

19.1 Personal representatives

We have seen that personal representatives are under a duty to:

- finalize the deceased's tax affairs
- settle any outstanding liabilities which arose during the deceased's lifetime
- probably, submit an Inheritance Tax account to enable probate or letters of administration to be granted.

When a person dies, there may be tax owed by the deceased to the Revenue or the other way round. Personal representatives are under a duty to make sure that all tax properly due is paid and all repayments or overpayments received and accounted for. In every case, it is necessary to distinguish between tax before death and tax arising after death and to remember that the tax year is not the calendar year but runs from 6 April to 5 April next.

19.1.1 Income Tax

a The deceased's income before death

All personal representatives must submit a Return to the Revenue of the deceased's income up to the date of death as soon as possible following the death. As soon as you know that you are a personal representative, you should write to the deceased's tax office to report the death, request a Return and ask whether any tax is or may be owed by or to the deceased's estate. Always quote the deceased's tax reference number if you know it. If you do not, give his or her full name and address and, if possible, National Insurance number. A model letter is set out below.

---

49 Maradon Crescent
Cornford
1 June 2003   Loamshire
                                              CD7 2BG

Cornford Area Tax Office
Cornford House
High Road
Cornford
Loamshire CD1 1FT

Dear Sirs

URSULA BENTHAM DECEASED FORMERLY OF 22
MAIN STREET CORNFORD, LOAMSHIRE – TAX
REFERENCE NUMBER: 262/98391

I am an executor of the will of Ursula Bentham, who died
on the 30 April 2003, jointly with Mrs Bentham's sister,
Veronica Strange. I enclose a copy of the death certificate
for your records.

Would you please tell me if any tax was owed by or to
Mrs Bentham at the date of her death and let me have
details of your calculations?

Would you also please let me have a Return for the period
ended on the day of Mrs Bentham's death? It would help
us to complete that Return if you could send me a copy of
Mrs Bentham's last Return.

Yours faithfully

Jeremy Watts

Under current legislation, you can claim full personal reliefs on
behalf of the deceased for the tax year in question; there is no
adjustment to take account of the death.

Example

Harry, a wealthy widower aged 81, dies on 31 May 2003. His personal representatives are entitled to claim his full personal relief and age allowance for the tax year ending 5 April 2004.

b The deceased's continuing income

It often happens that a person receives income from a source that does not stop on death such as rent, dividends or interest. In these circumstances, the receipt of such income after death is treated for tax purposes as income received by the deceased's estate. It should therefore not be included in the Return of the deceased's pre-death income.

Similarly, if the deceased had a life interest in a trust (see Chapter 07) any income arising before death, but not paid until after it, is treated as income of the estate and should not be included in the Return of the deceased's pre-death income.

c Overpayment and underpayments of Income Tax

Unless the affairs of the deceased are very straightforward, it is unlikely that you will be able to state exactly how much income tax was owed by or to the deceased at the date of death. As we have seen, personal representatives cannot obtain a grant of probate or letters of administration until any Inheritance Tax due in respect of the deceased's estate has been paid. Neither the personal representatives nor the beneficiaries will want the administration of the estate to be delayed by the failure to obtain the grant so it is now common practice to make an informed estimate of Income Tax owed to or by the estate and include that estimate figure in the appropriate Inheritance Tax account.

d Estate income

By 'estate income', we mean income received by the deceased's estate during the administration period. This period starts on the day after death and finishes on the day when the value of the residuary estate is calculated for distribution purposes.

Personal representatives must pay income tax on income received by the estate during the administration period. Unlike taxpayers who are alive, personal representatives cannot claim personal reliefs. The quid pro quo for this is that estate income is not liable to higher rate tax, which is currently 40%. Relief is available for interest paid in the first 12 months of any loan raised to pay Inheritance Tax.

19.1.2 Capital Gains Tax

a The deceased's capital gains before death

The position is broadly the same as Income Tax. The personal representatives must settle any Capital Gains Tax payable for gains made during the deceased's lifetime. They can claim full reliefs and exemptions for the tax year in question.

Example

Harry dies on 31 July 2003. On 12 May 2003, he sold shares, which resulted in a gain of £8,300. Harry's personal representative can claim the full relief for the tax year ending 5 April 2004.

Gain:	£8,300
Less exempt amount	£7,900
Taxable gain	£ 400

---

b The deceased's capital losses before death

If the deceased has losses allowable for Capital Gains Tax purposes in the tax year of his death, his personal representatives may set those against any chargeable gains. If, after doing that, there are allowable losses left over (because the gains in the tax year of death are not big enough to absorb all the losses) the personal representatives may carry back any for up to three tax years and set them against any chargeable gains in those years. This may result in a tax repayment, which will be an asset of the estate. But, if the losses cannot be used up by 'carrying back', they cannot be carried forward and used by the personal representatives to set against any chargeable gains made during the administration period.

c Estate gains

Death is not an event which triggers a charge to Capital Gains Tax. In fact, something quite useful happens on death. The personal representatives are treated as acquiring the deceased's assets at their market value at the date of death. Thus, an asset which is 'pregnant' with a chargeable gain loses that element on the death of the owner.

Sales of the deceased's assets by his personal representative during the administration period may result in a chargeable gain or an allowable loss. In the case of a gain, Capital Gains Tax is payable by the personal representatives in the usual way. Personal representatives can claim the same exemptions as a living taxpayer and additional relief in the form of a proportion of the probate valuation costs. The gain is calculated by reference to the market value of the asset at the date of death. In the year of death only, personal representatives are allowed to claim relief for disposals made by the deceased **and** for the disposals made by themselves during the administration period.

Example

Godfrey dies on 16 September 2003. He held shares in FGH plc., which he bought as 'penny shares' some years earlier. These were valued at £25,000 at the date of his death. On 16 January 2004, his personal representatives sell these shares for £50,000 in order to raise money to pay legacies and repay a loan. This results in the following chargeable gain:

sale price		£50,000
LESS		
'base value'	£25,000	
probate valuation expenses	£ 200	
personal representatives' annual exemption	£ 7,900	
Godfrey's annual exemption	£ 7,900	£41,000
chargeable gain		£9,000

Personal representatives are also allowed (as a concession) to claim the main residence exemption when they sell a home that has been used as a main residence, provided that certain conditions are complied with.

d Estate losses

Allowable losses resulting from sales by personal representatives can only be used by them; they cannot be carried back and set against chargeable gains incurred by the deceased or carried forward and set against chargeable gains incurred by the beneficiaries.

If the personal representatives sell land or publicly quoted shares within one year of death at a price less than their market value at the date of death, the lower value may be substituted for the higher value for Inheritance Tax purposes with the result that some Inheritance Tax may be repaid. The lower value will also be treated as the base value for the purpose of calculating any subsequent gain for Capital Gains Tax purposes.

19.1.3 Inheritance Tax

a Introduction

In Chapter 07, we looked at the basic principles of Inheritance Tax and the main exemptions and reliefs available to taxpayers. In this section, we will look at:

- how to calculate the amount of Inheritance Tax payable on death
- how to value property for Inheritance Tax purposes
- who is liable to pay any Inheritance Tax that is due
- on which of the deceased's assets the burden of Inheritance Tax falls
- accounts and payment of Inheritance Tax.

d How to calculate the Inheritance Tax

Three steps need to be taken to calculate whether Inheritance Tax is payable on death and, if it is, how much.

Step 1: identify the estate

This sounds like another silly question but it is not. Broadly speaking, Inheritance Tax is payable on the value of all the property that the deceased owned outright at his death. This includes property passing under his will or under the intestacy rules, as well as property held under a joint tenancy and nominated property. Thus, property held by the deceased as a trustee in trust for someone else is excluded. So are the proceeds of a life insurance policy (where the deceased paid the premiums) payable to someone else.

There are two important exceptions to this general rule:

a Where the deceased had a life interest under a trust that ends on his death.

> **Example**
>
> By his will, Thomas appoints Alan and Benjamin to be the trustees of a trust under which the income is paid to Thomas's daughter, Ursula, during her life. On her death, the trust comes to an end and the trust fund is split equally between Thomas's grandchildren then living.
>
> On Ursula's death, her taxable estate includes the value of the trust fund even though she had no control over the capital of the fund, only the right to receive its income.

b Where the deceased retained an interest in property that he had given away. These are sometimes referred to by their technical name 'gifts with a reservation of benefit'.

> **Example**
>
> In 1997, Frances gave her house, then worth £150,000, to her two children but continued to live in it rent free until her death in 2002. On Frances's death, the house was valued at £300,000. Because she had retained an interest in the house by continuing to live there until she died, the house is treated as part of Frances's taxable estate, even though it is owned by her two children.

In the unlikely event of two people dying in circumstances where it is impossible to determine the order of death, they are treated for Inheritance Tax purposes as having died at the same time. The implications of this will become clear from the following illustration.

> **Example**
>
> David aged 23 and Sarah aged 25 are killed in a climbing accident. It is impossible to decide who died first. David and Sarah made wills leaving everything to each other.
>
> For property inheritance purposes, David survived Sarah so that his property, which now includes hers, passes under the intestacy rules to his parents. For Inheritance Tax purposes, Sarah's property passes to David and is taxable in the normal way. When David's property passes to his parents, Sarah's property is excluded from the property then liable to Inheritance

Tax. If Sarah and David were husband and wife, no Inheritance Tax would be payable on the passing of Sarah's property to David (transfers between spouses being exempt). On David's death, Sarah's property would be excluded from the charge to Inheritance Tax.

Step 2: value the estate
We deal with this on pages 144–5.

Step 3: claim exemptions and reliefs
Whether this or that exemption or relief is available depends upon the identity of the person who is entitled to the property on death. Thus:

(i) No Inheritance Tax will be payable if the person entitled is:

- the spouse of the deceased
- a charity
- a political party
- some national bodies, e.g. Museums and Art Galleries.

(ii) Inheritance Tax may be avoided in whole or in part if the property in question is business property or agricultural property.

(iii) Inheritance Tax at a reduced rate will be payable if the deceased received any property upon which Inheritance Tax has already been paid within five years before his death. This is 'tapering relief' referred to on page 52.

Example
Joan, a widow, leaves her estate worth £350,000 to her son Keith. Keith dies three years later leaving his estate, worth £550,000, to his two best friends. On Keith's death, Inheritance Tax is calculated in the normal way and the amount of Inheritance Tax reduced by a percentage of the tax paid on Joan's death.

(iv) Inheritance Tax may be payable where the deceased has died within seven years of making a lifetime gift. If Inheritance Tax becomes payable in respect of such a gift, it is best to seek professional advice about how much is payable and who is liable to pay it.

c How to value for Inheritance Tax purposes

The general rule is that the value of each of the deceased's assets is its open market value. In other words, it is the price that the asset might reasonably be expected to sell at in the open market immediately before death.

There are a number of special rules relating to the valuation of certain types of property. The most important of these rules relate to:

- *Quoted securities.* These are valued by reference to the prices quoted in the Stock Exchange Official Daily List for the date of death. If the Stock Exchange was closed on that date, the valuation is by reference to the prices quoted on the nearest trading day before or after the date of death. The List shows two prices and the date of death. The value is usually taken as the lower value plus one-quarter of the difference between the two values.

Example

Simon owned 250 ABC plc ordinary 25p shares, which were quoted '150–158' in the Official List on the date of his death. The value of each share for Inheritance Tax purposes will therefore be 152p; i.e. 150 + (8÷4).

If you cannot face carrying out your own valuation, you can ask the deceased's bankers or any stock broker to do this. A fee will of course be payable for this service. Alternatively, you can obtain valuations online from www.sharedata.co.uk/valuations-head.html.

- *Unquoted securities*: the valuation of any unquoted security is a minefield for the unwary and it is best to obtain professional advice about this.
- *Land*: if the deceased owned land jointly with someone other than a spouse, the Revenue will normally allow the open market value to be reduced by 10%. Land owned jointly by spouses is not eligible for this allowance.
- *Life policies* to which the deceased was beneficially entitled: the value is the proceeds of the policy payable on death.

- *Liabilities*: these include:
  - any outstanding tax such as Inheritance Tax in respect of a lifetime transfer
  - mortgages
  - the deceased's reasonable funeral expenses
  - by Inland Revenue concession, the reasonable costs of a tombstone
  - money owed to a third party, for example a bank overdraft, credit/store card balance or payments under HP/credit sale agreements.

In certain circumstances, the value of an asset may be adjusted upwards or downwards by the Revenue or by the taxpayer. An example of this is where quoted securities are sold within 12 months of death for a figure lower than the date of death valuation. This may result in a reduction in the amount of any Inheritance Tax payable.

d Who is liable to pay Inheritance Tax?

The rules about liability for payment of Inheritance Tax arising on a transfer of assets on death are different from those relating to liability for lifetime transfers.

On transfers on death, the following are the main categories of persons who are all liable for Inheritance Tax attributable to that transfer:

- The personal representatives of the deceased to the extent of the assets they have received or are under their control.
- The trustees of a trust created by the deceased during his lifetime to the extent of any tax attributable to the assets they have received or are under their control.
- Any beneficiary under the deceased's will or the intestacy rules to the extent of any tax attributable to the assets they have received.
- Sometimes, buyers of property from personal representatives.

e Paying Inheritance Tax

Personal representatives will not be able to obtain probate or letters of administration without first paying any Inheritance Tax that is due when the Inland Revenue account is delivered to the Probate Registry. The problem here is often that the money needed to pay the Inheritance Tax is held by the deceased's bank or building society, who will not release it to the personal representatives without first seeing evidence of their title in the form of the grant of probate or of letters of administration. There are three ways of dealing with this situation:

(i) Borrowing

It may be possible to borrow the amount of Inheritance Tax from the deceased's bankers or the personal representatives' bankers. This will depend upon how well you know your bank or the deceased's bank who will need to be certain that the loan will be repaid without delay. Interest will of course be payable so it is important to ensure that the bank is clearly instructed to set up the facility as a loan and not as an overdraft otherwise income tax relief on the interest will not be available.

Alternatively, a beneficiary may be prepared to lend personal representatives the money needed to pay the Inheritance Tax either free of charge or at a rate lower than that charged by a commercial lender.

(ii) Payment

The deceased's bank or building society will usually agree to pay the Revenue direct, even though probate or letters of administration have not been granted. Since the end of March 2003 the Capital Taxes office has put in place a scheme whereby personal representatives can draw on money held in the deceased(s) account(s) to pay Inheritance Tax due on the form IHT 200 (see page 150).

(iii) Selling assets

It may be possible for executors (but not usually administrators) to sell quoted investments or other items, such as a car or jewellery, to raise the money needed to pay the Inheritance Tax. Under Stock Exchange rules as they now stand, an executor can sell quoted investments before probate is granted, although he will have to show probate to the buyer in due course.

f Burden of Inheritance Tax

If Inheritance Tax is payable on death, the personal representatives are faced with the question of deciding what property in the deceased's estate should be sold in order to pay the tax. The answer to this question depends largely upon whether the deceased made a valid will or not.

The general rule is that Inheritance Tax is payable out of the deceased's residuary estate unless the will says otherwise. For example, the deceased may have gifted money or possessions 'subject to Inheritance Tax' or words to that effect. In these circumstances, it is clear that the gifted property is burdened with its own Inheritance Tax so that the recipient of the gift must pay the bill. Where the gift is expressed to be 'free of Inheritance Tax' or words to that effect, any Inheritance Tax attributable to the gifted property will be payable from the proceeds of sale of some other property of the deceased.

As we have seen, no grant can be obtained unless the personal representatives have paid any Inheritance Tax due. This may mean that personal representatives have paid Inheritance Tax attributable to an item of property that the deceased intended should bear its own tax; for example, where property is gifted 'subject to Inheritance Tax'. In these circumstances, personal representatives have a right to reclaim the amount of tax they have paid in respect of the gift from the recipient of it.

Problems can occur where the deceased makes tax free gifts to beneficiaries who are not liable to pay Inheritance Tax, such as spouses or charities. If you are faced with dealing with this situation, it is best to obtain professional advice.

g Accounts and payment

The general rule is that the deceased's personal representatives must submit an account to the Revenue within 12 months of the end of the month in which the deceased died. Thus, if Godfrey died on 16 July 2002, the deadline for the account to reach the Revenue is 31 July 2003 not 16 July 2003.

The general rule is that Inheritance Tax is due and payable within six months after the end of the month in which the death occurred. Inheritance Tax paid late is liable to interest (from the due date to the actual date of payment), which does not qualify for Income Tax relief.

In certain cases, the taxpayer – usually the personal representatives – has the right to pay Inheritance Tax by annual equal instalments over a ten-year period. The most common examples of this right are in relation to land (where interest on the outstanding tax is always payable) or on a business interest (where interest on the outstanding tax will not be payable provided that the tax is paid on time).

19.2 Completing the Inheritance Tax accounts

We now look at the two Inheritance Tax accounts, one of which you will need to complete before probate or letters of administration can be granted. These forms can be downloaded from the Internet (www.inlandrevenue.gov.uk/cto) and are also available from Probate Registries. The factor that determines the type of account is the size of the estate.

19.2.1 General

The Inheritance Tax account does four things:

- It is an inventory of everything the deceased owned outright or is treated for Inheritance Tax purposes as having owned at the date of death.
- It is statement of debts and liabilities at the date of death.
- It is a claim form for Inheritance Tax exemptions and reliefs.
- It contains the calculations for the amount of any Inheritance Tax that is payable.

Personal representatives must bear in mind that they are under a strict duty to make the fullest enquiries reasonably practicable about the deceased's affairs. This means (amongst other things) that you must be able to back up the figures contained in the relevant account. Do not try to fob the Revenue off; this could land you in serious trouble. If, after making your enquiries, you are still not sure about the value of an asset or liability, you should telephone the Capital Taxes Office Helpline on 0115 774 2400 and ask them how to proceed.

19.2.2 Form Inheritance Tax 205

This account should be used where:

- the deceased died domiciled in the UK
- there is no trust property in the estate
- the gross value of the estate at the date of death did not exceed a specified sum, currently £220,000
- the gross value of any property outside the UK did not exceed £75,000
- the deceased made no transfers of assets chargeable to Inheritance Tax within the seven-year period before his death.

If any of these conditions cannot be satisfied, you must complete a different form, Inheritance Tax 200 – see page 150.

You will see that form IHT 205 is divided into Parts A and B:

a General questions

These are set out on page 2 (Part A) to enable the Revenue to decide whether you are completing the correct form or not. You will find that we have addressed the subject matter of these questions, except question 5, in this book. Question 5 is concerned with the ownership of property outside the UK. (For the purposes of this account, the UK does not include the Channel Islands and the Isle of Man.) If the deceased held any such assets, you should include their value in the account but obtain professional advice about how to deal with them.

b Statement of assets

Questions 3 to 8 on page 3 (Part A) set out clearly the nature and identity of the asset under consideration. Always include the original valuation where you have obtained this.

c Debts and liabilities

These are set out on page 4 (Part A). In answer to the question about mortgage debts, you should include only the deceased's share of the loan.

Example

Elizabeth and her husband Frederick own Honeysuckle Cottage as joint tenants. On Elizabeth's death, the house is worth £150,000 and there is a mortgage of £50,000 over it. Elizabeth's executors show £25,000 of mortgage debt in question 19. (The corresponding figure for question 16 is £75,000.) If Elizabeth and Frederick owned Honeysuckle Cottage as tenants in common in the proportions of 75% for Elizabeth and 25% for Frederick, the figures would be £37,500 for question 19 and £112,500 for question 16.

---

d Tax Calculation

The calculations at the end of question 19 on page 4 should reveal that the net value of the deceased's estate is less than £220,000 so that no Inheritance Tax is payable.

19.2.3 Form Inheritance Tax 200

You must use this account if any of the conditions for using form IHT 205 cannot be complied with. If the Probate Registry did not send you form IHT 200 with their package, ask them to send it to you now or download it from the Internet.

You will find form IHT 200 is longer than form IHT 205 and the questions it asks are more detailed. Fortunately, the Capital Taxes Office publishes a set of helpful notes – booklet IHT 200 User Guide – which we recommend.

19.3 Beneficiaries

Recipients of gift made by will or under the intestacy rules may be liable to tax during the administration period and/or after it.

19.3.1 Income Tax

We saw in the first section of this chapter that estate income is liable to Income Tax. This income is collected by the personal representatives and then distributed to the beneficiaries according to the terms of the will or under the intestacy rules.

If you are the recipient of estate income, you should include it in your Return for the relevant tax year. The personal representatives should give you a tax deduction certificate, which you should send to the Revenue with your Return for the relevant tax year. The result of doing that will depend upon your personal circumstances so that:

- if you are not liable to income tax, you will be able to claim a repayment of all the tax deducted
- if you are a basic rate taxpayer, your liability to pay Income Tax at the basic rate has been discharged by the personal representatives, so you will not have to pay Income Tax or
- if you are a higher rate (40%) taxpayer, your liability to pay Income Tax on that income is at the rate of difference depending on the rate of tax that has been deducted.

It sometimes happens that a beneficiary is not sure in which tax year the income has arisen and, therefore, is liable to be taxed. Furthermore, it may sometimes be difficult to decide whether a payment is one of capital or of income. If these questions arise, it is best to obtain professional advice about them.

19.3.2 Capital Gains Tax

The disposal by personal representatives of the deceased's assets in accordance with the will or under the intestacy rules does not operate as a taxable event for Capital Gains Tax purposes. Beneficiaries are regarded as having acquired their property at a value arrived at by the following formula:

Market value of asset at date of death

+

benefit of indexation allowance between date of death and date of transfer

+

proportion of transfer costs (if any)

Example

Juliet owned 750 shares in PQR plc., which she bought for £3,500. By her will, she gave them to her friend, Keith. The market value of these shares at the date of her death was £5,000. Their value had increased to £7,500 at the time of their transfer to Keith. The benefit of indexation allowance was £275 and the transfer costs were £50. Keith is treated as having acquired the shares for £5,325 calculated as follows:

£5,000 + £275 + £50 = £5,325

19.3.3 Inheritance Tax

We considered liability to Inheritance Tax on pages 145–6.

20

administering the estate

In this chapter you will learn:
- about collecting the assets
- about the payment of debts and other liabilities
- about the protection of personal representatives
- about missing beneficiaries
- about the change of entitlement after death.

In this Chapter we look at the steps that should be taken, following the issue of probate or of letters of administration, to progress the administration of a solvent estate.

20.1 Asset collection

Now that the grant has been issued, you must start to collect in the assets if you have not already begun this process. If you have done so already, you should open a bank account to receive monies owing to the estate. Your bank or the deceased's bank should do this. You will also need to write to the deceased's bank, building society and others to register the grant. You will find model letters to a bank or building society, an insurance company and company registrar in the examples on the following pages.

49 Maradon Crescent
Cornford
[Date]   Loamshire
CD7 2BG

Barwest Bank Plc
28 High Street
Cornford
Loamshire
CD1 5TD

Your Ref: 0123456

Dear Sirs

**URSULA BENTHAM DECEASED: ACCOUNT
NUMBERS 0123456 and 9876543**

Probate has now been granted and we enclose an office
copy of it for noting in your records.

Will you now please close these accounts; send us final
statements and your cheque for the closing balances made
payable to 'the personal representatives of Ursula Bentham
deceased'.

Yours faithfully

....

Jeremy Watts   Veronica Strange

model letter to bank or building society

49 Maradon Crescent
Cornford
Loamshire
CD7 2BG

[Date]

Fortitude Mutual Life Company
Temperance House
High Road
London
NW12 6PF

BY RECORDED DELIVERY

Dear Sirs

URSULA BENTHAM DECEASED: POLICY NUMBER
456789

Probate has now been granted and we enclose:

1 An office copy of the grant for noting in your records;

2 Policy Number 456789.

Please acknowledge receipt and let us have your cheque for
the policy proceeds, together with interest from the date of
death until date of payment, made payable to 'The personal
representatives of Ursula Bentham deceased'. Please also let
us have a statement showing how this payment has been
calculated.

Yours faithfully

....

Jeremy Watts   Veronica Strange

model letter to insurance company

49 Maradon Crescent
Cornford
[Date]
Loamshire
CD7 2BG

Registrars' Department
Barwest Bank Plc
The Causeway
Northend on Sea
ND99 4PX

Dear Sirs

URSULA BENTHAM DECEASED

Probate has now been granted to us and we enclose an office copy of it for noting in your records. We will let you know shortly to whom the shares are to be transferred.

Please send us your cheque for dividends unpaid made payable to 'The personal representatives of Ursula Bentham deceased' as soon as possible.

Yours faithfully

....

Jeremy Watts   Veronica Strange

model letter to company registrar

If the deceased was owed any money (other than under a mortgage) this should be collected now and paid in to the personal representatives' account.

If the deceased was involved in any court proceedings, you must take legal advice about how to proceed.

20.2 Payment of debts and other liabilities

The detailed enquiries that you made to complete the Inheritance Tax account should give you a full picture of the deceased's debts and liabilities. These will include funeral expenses. You will know whether any assets will need to be sold or if the debts and liabilities can be settled out of money in hand. If there is insufficient cash in the estate to meet all the liabilities, you must consult with the beneficiaries about which assets are to be sold. Remember that the sale of an asset may have capital gains tax implications, which should be worked through before any steps are taken to sell.

Debts and liabilities should normally be paid or settled as soon as possible after death. Sometimes a will says that debts should be paid late (for example, at the end of the administration period). You should ignore provisions like this because they are not legally enforceable.

There are complex rules laid down by Parliament about the order in which the estate assets may be used (i.e. sold) to pay debts. This book is not the place to review and comment upon those rules. The form of will that we have used in this book does, we believe, identify the property that must be used to pay debts and, in effect, overrule those statutory provisions. Where there is no will or where the will under which you are appointed says nothing about the payment of debts and liabilities, which are substantial, you should obtain professional advice about how to proceed.

20.3 Protection of personal representatives

The law says that personal representatives are personally liable for the valid claim of any unpaid beneficiary or creditor even if they knew nothing of the claim. Fortunately, the law also provides the means of protection from such claims. This takes the form of a notice which requires claimants to send details of their claim to the personal representatives. Claimants have two months in which to do this. After the end of that period, the personal representatives may safely distribute the estate on the basis of claims received by them. A model form of notice for executors is set out opposite. Administrators can use the same form, changing the references from 'executors' to 'administrators'.

TRUSTEE ACT 1925 SECTION 27

Ursula Bentham Deceased

PLEASE TAKE NOTICE that any person having a claim against or an interest in the estate of Ursula Bentham deceased formerly of 22 Main Street Cornford Loamshire who died on 30 April 2003 must send written particulars of it to her executors at 49 Maradon Crescent Cornford Loamshire CD7 2BG before 3 October 2003. After that date, the executors will proceed to distribute the deceased's assets among those entitled, having regard only to those claims or interests notified to them before 3 October 2003.

Dated 2 July 2003

Jeremy Watts and Veronica Strange
executors of the will of Ursula Bentham deceased.

The law does not make an advertisement obligatory but if there is any doubt in your mind about the identity or whereabouts of any of the beneficiaries or creditors of the estate, you should advertise. If you are an executor, there is no reason why you cannot advertise before the issue of the grant of probate; this will speed up the administration process. If you are an administrator, you cannot really do this because your legal authority to act as personal representative does not come into existence until the grant of letters of administration.

The advertisement must normally be placed in:

- *The London Gazette* and
- a local newspaper circulating in the area in which the deceased lived.

20.4 Missing beneficiaries

If you find yourself in the position of being unable to locate a missing beneficiary, you should obtain legal advice about how the estate is to be administered.

20.5 Change of entitlement after death

There are a number of ways in which beneficial entitlement can be changed after death. These alterations have tax and inheritance implications and should not be undertaken without all the parties involved taking suitable professional advice.

The most common method of changing beneficial entitlement after death is by means of a Deed of Variation or, as it is sometimes called, a Deed of family arrangement. This deed can be used to change who gets what under a will or under the intestacy rules. Provided that all the beneficiaries are in agreement, the deceased's estate can be distributed as the beneficiaries want. If any of the beneficiaries are children under the age of 18, the approval of the courts to the variation will be required. This can be a lengthy and expensive process.

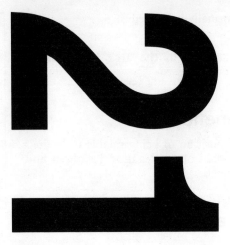

2 1

distribution

In this chapter you will learn:
- about non-residuary gifts of money
- about non-residuary gifts of land
- about non-residuary gifts of property other than money and land
- about tax adjustments and clearances
- how to prepare estate accounts
- how to distribute the residue.

In this chapter, we look at what needs to be done to distribute and wind up a straightforward solvent estate.

The distribution process can begin once the debts and liabilities, including the funeral expenses, have been paid (or at least provided for).

21.1 Non-residuary gifts of money

The deceased's will, if it has been drawn up properly, should make it clear who the beneficiaries are and how much each of them is to receive. If there is any doubt about the existence or identity of a beneficiary or the amount of the gift, you should obtain legal advice.

The will should also be checked carefully to see what the testator said about the property to be sold to pay the cash gifts. Normally, such gifts are payable out of the property, which consists of the deceased's residuary estate, but this is not always so. If the will does not say where cash gifts are to be paid from, you should seek legal advice.

As a general rule, non-residuary case gifts should be paid not later than one year after the testator's death. Sometimes, this is not possible and, if payment is delayed beyond the 'executors' year', the beneficiary is entitled to be paid interest until payment is made.

21.2 Non-residuary gifts of land

Again, if there is any doubt about the existence or identity of a beneficiary or the land in question, you should obtain legal advice.

Title to land is transferred to a beneficiary by means of a document known as an assent, which must be in one of the forms prescribed by Her Majesty's Land Registry. This can be obtained from any law stationers or downloaded from the Internet (www.landreg.gov.uk).

If the beneficiary is a child under 18 years old, the assent must be made to trustees on his behalf. As we have seen, a minor cannot hold legal title to land. Such an assent is best prepared by qualified conveyancers.

21.3 Other non-residuary gifts

These include gifts of personal possessions and investments.

21.3.1 Personal possessions

These can normally be transferred to the beneficiary by handing them over to him. You should obtain a receipt from the beneficiary, which will have the effect in law of discharging you from your obligations to him. The following is a suitable form of receipt.

URSULA BENTHAM DECEASED

I acknowledge receipt of [description of item] from Jeremy Watts and Veronica Strange the personal representatives of Ursula Bentham, deceased.

Signature of beneficiary: date:

In the case of a beneficiary under 18, their parents or guardian should be asked to give a receipt on behalf of their child.

21.3.2 Investments

Quoted and unquoted securities should be transferred to a beneficiary by a document called a stock transfer form, which you can obtain from law stationers. The completed form, the share certificate and (if not already sent) the original or an office copy of the grant (but not a certified photocopy) should then be sent to the registrars of the company concerned with a request to issue a new certificate in the name of the beneficiary. An example of a suitable form of letter is on page 164.

Special forms are required for withdrawals and transfer of National Savings certificates and National Savings accounts. All these can be obtained from the office concerned. Premium Bonds can no longer be transferred; they must be cashed in.

21.4 Tax adjustments and clearances

21.4.1 Income Tax and Capital Gains Tax

In Chapter 19, we saw that personal representatives must submit Returns for the tax years, or parts of them, in which the deceased died and in which the administration of his estate is carried out.

At the end of the administration period, the personal representatives should write to the Inspector at the deceased's tax district to obtain confirmation that they have made all payments of Income Tax and Capital Gains Tax that they are required to make and that no further payments from them are due.

21.4.2 Inheritance Tax

We also saw in Chapter 19 that adjustments to the amount of Inheritance Tax payable could be made for various reasons. Major adjustments (upwards or downwards) should be reported to the Capital Taxes Office immediately. There is a special form (C4) for doing this that can be obtained from the Capital Taxes Office or its website (www.inlandrevenue.gov.uk). If any such adjustments come to light, you should seek professional advice.

Minor adjustments should also be reported to the Capital Taxes Office as soon as they occur. These can normally be dealt with by letter.

When you are satisfied that all the Inheritance Tax for which you are responsible has been paid, you should apply to the Capital Taxes Office for a discharge. This is done by submitting a special form (IHT 30) to the Capital Taxes Office. IHT 30 contains a summary of the accounts previously submitted and details of the Inheritance Tax paid. If the Revenue is satisfied that no further Inheritance Tax is due and payable, they will issue a certificate that discharges you from your liability. If you have elected to pay Inheritance Tax by instalments, the Revenue will issue a limited discharge so that you should apply for full discharge when the last instalment has been paid.

49 Maradon Crescent
Cornford
Loamshire
CD7 2BG

[Date]

Registrars' Department
Barwest Bank Plc
The Causeway
Northend on Sea
ND99 4PX

BY RECORDED DELIVERY

Your Ref:

Dear Sirs

URSULA BENTHAM DECEASED

Probate has now been granted and we enclose:

1 Share certificate number
2 Office copy of the probate*
3 Stock transfer form.

Please acknowledge receipt and send the new share certificate in the name of [beneficiary] to us here.

Yours faithfully

....

Jeremy Watts   Veronica Strange

* Note: if not previously sent.

21.5 Preparing estate accounts

This is the final task for executors or administrators.

The purpose of the accounts is to show all the deceased's assets and how these were used. The accounts should contain a full record of assets received and how they were used to pay legacies, funeral expenses, debts and other liabilities. They should also show the balance is paid to the residuary beneficiaries. It is customary to ask the beneficiaries to indicate their approval of the accounts by signing them. The effect of such signing is to discharge the executors or administrators from their duties to supply any further accounts to the beneficiaries unless there is fraud or failure to disclose assets.

There is no special way of preparing estate accounts. They should be as clear and consise as possible. An example follows.

URSULA BENTHAM DECEASED

EXECUTORS' STATEMENT

By her will dated 30 September 2002, the late Ursula Bentham appointed her son Jeremy Watts and her sister Veronica Strange to be the executors and trustees of her estate. Mrs Bentham died on 30 April 2003 and probate of her will was granted out of the Brighton District Probate Registry on 1 October 2003.

By her will, Mrs Bentham gave the following cash legacies:

1. £2,000 to Jane Stevens
2. £2,000 to Veronica Strange

and the residue of her estate to her son, Jeremy.

The net estate for probate purposes was £353,500; Inheritance Tax of £39,400 has been paid and a Certificate of Discharge obtained.

1. The estate at the date of death consisted of:

	£	£
22 Main Street Cornford (freehold)		260,000
House contents and personal effects		25,000
Investments in Schedule 1		50,000
Barwest Bank plc current account		2,000

Barwest Bank deposit account	20,000	
accrued interest	100	20,100
Pension arrears		100
Cash in house		50
The gross estate was therefore		357,250

2. The following liabilities existed at the date of death:

	£
Funeral expenses	2,000
Barwest Gold Card	1,050
Doctor's fees	450
Gas/Electricity	250
The Net Estate was therefore	353,500

3. Liabilities paid out of net estate

		£
Administration Expenses		
Inheritance Tax (Note A)	39, 400	
Valuers' fees	800	40,200
Legacies		
Jane Stevens	2,000	
Veronica Strange	2,000	4,000
		44,200

Note A: Mr Watts lent the executors this sum at no cost to the estate.

| The amount available for distribution (excluding income received after date of death) was therefore | 309,300 |

| 4. Income received by estate in Schedule 2 | 500 |

| The total amount available for distribution was therefore | 309,800 |

5. Beneficiary's account

| Distributable estate | 309,800 |
| Represented by the following assets transferred to you | |

Cash	50
22 Main Street Cornford	260,000
House contents and personal effects	25,000
Investments (balance)	22,800
Income arising (Schedule 2)	500
Cash deposits (balance)	1,450
	309,800

SCHEDULE 1

20,000 FGH plc ordinary 50p	25,000
7,200 Amity plc ordinary 50p	12,000
6,000 United Fortress plc ordinary 25p	10,000
1,500 Barwest Bank plc ordinary 25p	3,000
	50,000

SCHEDULE 2

<u>Dividends</u>

FGH plc	230
United Fortress plc	200
	430

<u>Interest</u>

Barwest Bank plc	70
	500

22

administering and distributing an estate in Northern Ireland

In this chapter you will learn:
- the differences for estates in Northern Ireland
- where to apply in Northern Ireland.

After four lengthy and detailed chapters dealing with the administration and distribution of estates in England and Wales, it may come as a relief to find a short chapter dealing with estates in Northern Ireland. Fortunately, the law relating to the administration and distribution of estates in Northern Ireland is broadly in line with that of England and Wales so that, in this chapter, we need only explain the main differences.

22.1 Appointment of executors

The law in Northern Ireland is the same as in England and Wales. The only difference is that the services of the Public Trustee are not available in Northern Ireland.

22.2 Gifts

If there is no evidence available about the order of death of husband and wife, the law in Northern Ireland does not assume that the older died first. Instead, both are treated as having died at the same time.

The order of death can become a matter of great importance and it is not unknown for 'disinherited' family members to ask for detailed forensic examinations, which can cause the deceased's close family great distress.

Because of the rule of 'simultaneous death' it is sensible to make all large gifts conditional upon the beneficiary surviving the testator by, say, 28 days.

22.3 Government stock valuation

Holders of Government stock living in Northern Ireland may register this with the Bank of Ireland (Registration Department) instead of the Bank of England. The stock certificate or interest warrant will show the location of the Register.

22.4 Probate forms

The relevant forms, which are the same as those in England and Wales, can be obtained from the Probate and Matrimonial Office of the Probate Division Royal Courts of Justice,

Chichester Street, Belfast. If the deceased lived in the counties of Londonderry, Fermanagh or Tyrone, the forms can be obtained from the District Office at 13 Bishop Street, Londonderry. At the time of writing, we were unable to find the forms on the Internet.

22.5 Protection of personal representatives

Personal representatives in Northern Ireland can protect themselves by advertisement in the same way as personal representatives in England and Wales (see pages 157–9). The advertisement must be placed in the *Belfast Gazette,* not the *London Gazette.*

22.6 Land

The principles of land transfer are broadly the same as those in England and Wales, with one important exception: whereas in England and Wales the title to all land must be registered at Her Majesty's Land Registry if this has not been done, there is no compulsory registration in Northern Ireland yet.

We suggest that transfers of land following death are dealt with by solicitors.

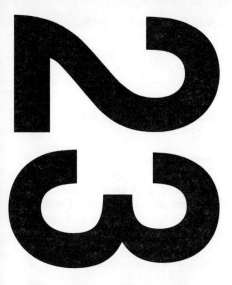

23
administering and distributing a Scottish estate

In this chapter you will learn:

- about the position of the personal representatives in Scotland
- how Scottish law looks on property
- the procedure for small estates in Scotland
- how to apply for confirmation where there is a will
- how to apply for confirmation where there is no will or no valid will
- about executors' powers and responsibilities
- how to distribute the estate.

There are significant differences between the law of England and Wales and the law of Scotland. These are noticeable in the legal vocabulary of Scotland and in the steps that need to be taken to administer an estate there.

23.1 Personal representatives in Scotland

In Scotland, all personal representatives are known as executors; the title of 'administrator' is unknown. An executor appointed by will is called an 'executor-nominate' and an executor of an estate of a person who has died without making a valid will or who has left no will at all is called an 'executor-dative'. Scottish law prescribes an order of applicants for the position of executor-dative. This applicant is usually a close member of the deceased's family. The application for appointment as executor-dative is normally handled by a solicitor.

In contrast to the position in England and Wales, the appointment of all executors, generally speaking, must be 'confirmed' by the Scottish courts before the executor can begin to deal with the administration of the deceased's estate. It follows that the authority of an executor to act pending confirmation is very limited; it is somewhat similar to that of a prospective administrator under the law of England and Wales. In other words, a Scottish executor should confine himself, pending confirmation, to safeguarding the deceased's property.

If an executor-nominate does not wish to act, he cannot be compelled to do so. If the deceased appointed other executors by his will, those who are willing to act may apply for their appointment to be confirmed, the renouncing executor being required to sign a statement that he does not wish to act. There is no special form for this. If a sole executor-nominate does not wish to act, he may either introduce a co-executor who is willing to do so and then refuse, or require the estate to be put to the trouble and expense of applying to the courts for an executor to be appointed.

23.2 How Scottish law regards property

In Scotland, property may be classified as heritable or moveable. Heritable property includes land and buildings; moveable property includes money, personal possessions, investments and bank and building society accounts. Both types of property may be owned by one person or more. Property owned by two or more persons may be held by them 'jointly' or 'in common'. It is more usual for property to be held 'in common', which is similar in many respects to the tenancy in common known to the law of England and Wales. Heritable property held in common by the deceased and others forms part of the deceased's estate to the extent of his interest in it. Such property passes under the will or in accordance with the intestacy rules unless the deeds contain a statement – known as a 'survivorship destination' – that it is to pass to the survivor of the co-owners.

The same can be said for moveable property. It is common for bank or building society accounts of married couples to be maintained as common property and operated on the basis that either of them can sign cheques during their lifetimes and that on first death the survivor can continue to operate the account. This arrangement does not regulate the ownership of the money in the account, which belongs to the account holder in the proportions in which they contributed, unless there is an intention to combine resources. No such intention is implied (or presumed) by Scottish law so it must be proved in the absence of clear supporting evidence.

23.3 Confirmation

The general rule is that confirmation is needed in all but the following cases:

- The property in the deceased's estate has been nominated. The rules are broadly the same as those in England and Wales; see pages 125–7.
- The only payments to be made to beneficiaries are small payments, currently not exceeding £5,000. The rules in Scotland are almost identical to those in England and Wales – see pages 125–7.
- The property owned by the deceased was held in common with others and there is a valid survivorship destination. In these circumstances, the deceased's interest passes directly to the survivor.

23.3.1 Procedure estate' of £25,000 or less

If the gross value of the deceased's estate is £25,000 or less, there is a special procedure for obtaining confirmation. There is no need to petition the court for the appointment of an executor and the court staff will complete the necessary forms.

a No will

If a deceased made no will or made a will that is not valid, the court must appoint an executor, usually someone who is entitled to inherit.

The intending executor must draw up a list of assets and liabilities (including the undertaker's account) stating their values and send it to the court where the information will be recorded on an official form (Form C1). The applicant will then be asked to attend court together with two witnesses who can assure the court that the applicant is who he says he is and who can verify his relationship to the deceased.

At this stage, the applicant will usually need to satisfy the court that he will be able to carry out his duties. This is done by obtaining a bond from an insurance company or sometimes from an individual of good financial standing for an amount equivalent to the gross value of the estate. This is known as a 'bond of caution'. Sometimes, insurance companies will refuse to issue bonds of caution to executors who wish to act for themselves. In these circumstances, the executors have no choice but to instruct solicitors to act on their behalf unless they can find a person of suitable financial standing to provide the bond.

Following the lodging of the bond of caution with the court, confirmation will be issued.

b Will

The procedure is similar to that outlined above, except that:

- The applicant must send that original will to the court at the same time as the lists of assets and liabilities. The will will be returned when confirmation is issued.
- No bond of caution is required.
- There is no need for independent witnesses to attend court when Form C1 is signed.

23.3.2 Procedure – estates over £25,000

In contrast to England and Wales, in Scotland there are no
special procedures or forms used by personal representatives
who wish to act personally without professional assistance. Nor
is any special provision made by the court to help such persons.

The following steps need to be taken:

Step 1

Complete the appropriate application forms(s). These can be
obtained from the Capital Taxes Office, HM Commissary Office
(see page 196 for address and telephone number), Sheriff Courts
and main post offices. Alternatively, they can be downloaded
from the Internet (www.inlandrevenue. gov.uk/cto).

Form C1

This is the form required to enable you to act as executor of the
deceased's estate. It must be completed whenever Confirmation
is required. The Inland Revenue publish a useful set of guidance
notes (Form C3) to help you to complete Form C1. Page 1 is
straightforward. Page 2 is more technical so if you get stuck
you should ask for help from either a solicitor or a Sheriff's
Court officer.

Pages 3 and 4 serve two functions. Together they comprise the
inventory of the deceased's estate and the Inland Revenue
account where the executor must disclose all property, whether
or not Inheritance Tax is payable by reason of the deceased's
death. All the deceased's assets, together with their values, must
be listed otherwise the form will be rejected.

Form IHT200

If the inventory in Form C1 shows that the gross value of the
deceased's estate exceeds £220,000 you will need to complete
Form IHT200. This form may also have to be completed, even
if the gross value is less than that figure if certain other
conditions are not satisfied. The guidance notes (Form C3)
explain in detail what these conditions are and when they apply.

As we said in Section 19.2.3 of Chapter 19, IHT200 is a long
form with many detailed questions. Fortunately, the Capital
Taxes office publishes a set of helpful notes – The IHT200 User
Guide – which we strongly recommend.

Step 2

Having completed Form C1, you must sign the declaration on page 2. If the will is holograph (see Chapter 12) you may need sworn statements from two people to the effect that the will is not a forgery.

Step 3 (where there is no will or no valid will)

We have seen that, if the deceased did not make a valid will or left no will at all, the Court must appoint an executor. This is normally dealt with by a solicitor. Furthermore, as an executor appointed by the Court, you will need to obtain a bond of caution – see page 174.

Step 4 (where Inheritance Tax is payable)

If you completed Form IHT200, it is likely that Inheritance Tax is payable. You should send the following documents to the Capital Taxes Office (see page 196 for addresses):

- Form IHT200 signed on the back page. The Capital Taxes office will check your calculations and then send you a receipt to show that all tax now due has been paid. You will need to send this to the Sheriff's Court – see below. The Inheritance Tax payable at this stage is a provisional amount and further tax may be payable or a refund made depending upon the value of the assets in the deceased's estate.
- A cheque for Inheritance Tax made payable to 'Inland Revenue'.

Final Step

The last step is to file the documents required for confirmation. These consist of:-

- the Capital Taxes Office's receipt for inheritance tax
- the will (and supporting documentation)
- if there is no will, the Court appointment and bond of caution
- a cheque for the prescribed fee.

All these documents should be sent (or handed in at) the appropriate Sheriff's Court. This is the court for the place of the deceased's residence at his death.

If the Court has a query, it will let you know. Otherwise, it will issue the confirmation and return the will, usually within 10 to 14 days of lodgement.

23.4 Executors' powers and duties

For most practical purposes these are broadly in line with those of executors in England and Wales.

23.5 Administering and distributing an estate

Once the confirmation has been issued, you can administer and distribute the estate in accordance with the will or the intestacy rules (see Chapter 16).

There are several material differences between the position of an executor of an English (or Welsh) estate and a Scottish estate including the following.

23.5.1 Unknown creditors

There is no provision under Scottish law that corresponds directly to Trustee Act 1925, Section 27 (see page 158). Instead, executors have the right to pay all known creditors and to distribute the deceased's estate to those beneficially entitled after six months has elapsed from the date of death. Any creditor who submits a late claim stands to lose his money if the estate has been distributed unless it can be proved that the executors should have known of the creditor's existence. Notwithstanding this protection, if there is any doubt in your mind about the nature and extent of the deceased's creditors, it is sensible to advertise the death in a newspaper circulating in the area where the deceased lived.

23.5.2 Unknown beneficiaries

As we have seen, the inheritance rules in Scotland are different to those in England and Wales. Great care must be taken to identify all possible claimants. If you are not certain of the identity of all the beneficiaries, or if any of them are under 16, you should obtain legal advice before proceeding any further.

23.5.3 Debts

After all the assets have been collected in, it is essential that all known debts are settled before any money is paid to the beneficiaries. Debts of a solvent estate must be paid in the following order:

- deathbed and reasonable funeral expenses
- secured debts; for example a mortgage
- preferred debts; for example taxes and National Insurance contributions
- ordinary debts.

Each category of debt must be paid in full before the next category. Within each category, each creditor is paid the same proportion if all the creditors cannot be paid in full.

When all the debts have been paid, you can distribute the estate to those beneficially entitled. Gifts of land are made by a document called a 'docket' unless the title deeds contain a survivorship destination to a beneficiary under the will or under the intestacy rules or who has prior legal rights. Sales, as distinct from gifts, are made by a document called a 'disposition'. We suggest that all land transactions are best handled by solicitors.

23.6 Insolvent estates

The position of a Scottish executor is broadly the same as an executor in the estate of England and Wales. If the estate is insolvent or appears to be insolvent, you should seek legal advice straightaway.

appendices

Appendix 01: Sample wills

SIMPLE WILL

THIS WILL is made by me [name] of [address]

1. I REVOKE any earlier will and codicil that I have made and declare this to be my last will.

2. I APPOINT [name] of [address] to be executor of this my will.

3. I GIVE all my property of every kind to [name] of [address] if [he] [she] survives me by 28 days. If [name of beneficiary] does not survive me by 28 days, my executor must dispose of all my property to such charity or charities as [he] [she] thinks fit.

4. I HAVE signed this will in witness of its provisions on this   day   of   2003

SIGNED by the [Testator] [Testatrix] in our joint presence }
                                                            }
and then by us together in [his] [hers]   }

WILL WITHOUT TRUSTS

THIS WILL is made by me [name] of [address]

1.1   I REVOKE any earlier will and codicil that I have made.

1.2   I DECLARE this will to be my last will.

2.   I APPOINT [name] of [address] and [name] of [address] to be the executors of this will.

3.   I GIVE free of inheritance tax [amount of money] to my friend [name] of [address].

4.   I GIVE free of inheritance tax [description of item] to my friend [name] of [address].

5.1   I GIVE to my Executors as joint tenants, free of inheritance tax, all my personal chattels as defined by section 55 (1) (x) of the Administration of Estates Act 1925.

5.2   I REQUEST my Executors, without imposing any sort of trust or binding obligation upon them or conferring any interest upon any other person, to dispose of my personal chattels in accordance with any letter of wishes of mine that may come to their attention within three (3) months of my death.

6.1   I GIVE all my property of every kind which is not disposed of by this will or any codicil to it to my Executors who must hold such property UPON TRUST to

   • sell the whole or any part of it or
   • retain the whole or any part of it in the same form as it was at the date of my death for as long as my Executors decide.

6.2   THE DECISION of my Executors whether to sell or to retain my property is a matter for them alone and they will not be liable for any loss caused as a result of the exercise of their discretion.

6.3   MY EXECUTORS must pay out of the monies arising from such sale:

- my funeral expenses
- any testamentary expenses
- any debts
- any legacies and
- any taxation payable on or by reason of my death.

and having done so hold what is left for:

- my wife [name] if she survives me but if she does not then
- my brother [name] of [address].

7. IN ADDITION to their statutory powers, my Executors may:

7.1 invest and change any investments freely as if they were beneficially entitled to them; and

7.2 hold investments in the name of any third party they think fit; and

8. FOR THE purposes of determining beneficial entitlement under this will:

8.1 any person who does not survive me by 28 days will be treated as having died before me;

8.2 the statutory and equitable rules of apportionment will not apply;

8.3 any payment in the nature of income received by my Executors is to be treated as income at the date of its receipt even if the whole or any part of such payment relates to a period before the date of my death.

9. I HAVE signed this will in witness of its provisions this day of   2003

SIGNED by the [Testator] [Testatrix] in our joint presence   }

                                                               }

and then by us together in [his] [hers]   }

WILL WITH TRUSTS

THIS WILL is made by me [name] of [address]

1.1 I REVOKE any earlier will and codicil that I have made.

1.2 I DECLARE this will to be my last will.

2.1 I APPOINT [name] of [address] and [name] of [address] to be the executors and the trustees of this will.

2.2 IN THIS WILL, the expression 'my Trustees' means my executors and where necessary the trustees for the time being of any trust created by this will.

3. I GIVE free of inheritance tax [amount of money] to my friend [name] of [address].

4. I GIVE free of inheritance tax [description of item] to my friend [name] of [address].

5.1 I GIVE to my Trustees as joint tenants, free of inheritance tax, all my personal chattels as defined by section 55 (1) (x) of the Administration of Estates Act 1925.

5.2 I REQUEST my Trustees, without imposing any sort of trust or binding obligation upon them or conferring any interest upon any other person, to dispose of my personal chattels in accordance with any letter of wishes of mine that may come to their attention within three (3) months of my death.

6.1 I GIVE all my property of every kind which is not disposed of by this will or any codicil to it to my Trustees who must hold such property UPON TRUST to

- sell the whole or any part of it or
- Retain the whole or any part of it in the same form as it was at the date of my death for as long as my Trustees decide.

6.2 THE decision of my Trustees whether to sell or to retain my property is a matter for them alone and they will not be liable for any loss caused as a result of the exercise of their discretion.

6.3 MY Trustees must pay out of the monies arising from such sale:

- my funeral expenses
- any testamentary expenses
- any debts
- any legacies and
- any taxation payable on or by reason of my death.

and having done so hold what is left upon trust for:

- my son [name] if he survives me and attains the age of 18 but if he does not then
- my brother [name] of [address].

7. IN ADDITION to their statutory powers, my Trustees may:

7.1 invest and change any investments freely as if they were beneficially entitled to them which includes the right to invest in unsecured or interest free loans or other non-income producing assets including property for occupation or use by a beneficiary; and

7.2 hold investments in the name of any third party they think fit; and

7.3 borrow money on the security of my residuary estate for any purpose; and

7.4 apply for the benefit of any beneficiary as my Trustees think fit the whole or any part of:

(a) the income from the part of my residuary estate to which that beneficiary is or may in the future be entitled;

(b) the capital to which that beneficiary is or may in the future be entitled and on becoming absolutely entitled such beneficiary must bring into account any payments received under this clause.

7.5 exercise the power of appropriation under section 41 Administration of Estates Act 1925 without obtaining any of the required consents.

8. FOR THE purposes of determining beneficial entitlement under this will:

8.1 any person who does not survive me by 28 days will be treated as having died before me;

8.2 the statutory and equitable rules of apportionment will not apply;

8.3 any payment in the nature of income received by my Trustees is to be treated as income at the date of its receipt even if the whole or any part of such payment relates to a period before the date of my death.

9. I HAVE signed this will in witness of its provisions this day of   2003

SIGNED by the [Testator] [Testatrix] in our joint presence   }
                                                               }
and then by us together in [his] [hers]   }

Appendix 02: Dealing with the undertaker and other formalities

In this Appendix, we look briefly at some important practical considerations relating to the legal side of bereavement. We deal first with the position in England, Wales and Northern Ireland and then in Scotland.

Registering the death

When a person dies, the doctor attending them will issue a certificate, which states the cause of death. If the death occurred suddenly or in unusual circumstances the doctor must tell a coroner who may (and in certain cases must) hold an inquest to establish the cause of death. At the conclusion of the inquest, the coroner will issue his verdict following which the death must be registered.

A death must normally be registered within five days of its occurrence. Registration must always be made in person at the office of the Registrar of Deaths for the district in which the death occurred. Where the death has been reported to the coroner, the death cannot be registered until the coroner has authorized this. Registration is usually by the deceased's next of kin but it does not have to be.

The death certificate

The Registrar of Deaths will issue two certificates: the so-called 'disposal' certificate to enable the body to be buried or cremated, and the death certificate, which confirms the registration. One copy of each of these certificates is issued free of charge and extra copies have to be paid for.

Arranging the funeral

As we have said, a body cannot be buried or cremated without a disposal certificate. Consequently, no firm funeral arrangements should be made until that certificate has been issued.

Normally, an undertaker is engaged to take care of the funeral arrangements. If you put the funeral in the hands of an undertaker he will need the disposal certificate. It is essential to obtain a clear estimate of what the funeral costs will be before engaging the undertaker's services. If there is insufficient money in the estate, you may end up paying for some or all of the costs of the funeral yourself.

The law does not make one person in particular responsible for funeral arrangements; normally these are handled by the deceased's next of kin or their personal representatives.

The undertaker will usually take care of all the funeral practicalities, including paying the expenses (which will have to be reimbursed) of the burial or cremation. The formalities of cremation are greater than those of burial and, therefore, more expensive.

The position in Scotland

The rules relating to registration of death are slightly different in Scotland.

The death must be registered within eight days of its occurrence by any person who can provide the Registrar of Deaths for the place where the death occurred with the information they need. No disposal certificate is required because the Registrar's death certificate serves the same purpose.

In Scotland, inquests are known as public enquiries.

Appendix 03: Living wills

The expression 'living will' is a misnomer. A living will is not a will in the strict sense at all; it does not deal with matters of inheritance and property and does not need to conform to a set of rigid statutory requirements. Indeed, at the time of going to press, there is no legislation dealing specifically with living wills.

By 'living wills', a person usually means a written advance statement, made while they are in possession of all their faculties, about their future medical treatment. We adopt that meaning here.

Living wills have become so important that, in 1994, the House of Lords Select Committee on Medical Ethics called for a code of practice for the medical profession about advance directives. This resulted in a code being published by the British Medical Journal in April 1995.

The courts have decided that a person may refuse medical treatment in advance if three conditions are satisfied:

- The person must be fully aware of the implications of his request.
- Such awareness must have come about through a proper understanding of the treatment and its consequences for the person.
- The person must have envisaged the situation that has come about.

It follows that an advance statement must be very carefully worded. There are a number of printed forms currently available. In order to be valid, the advance statement must be signed by its maker and should also be witnessed.

It is not possible to make a legally binding advance statement that the person wishes to be refused basic care; in other words, the essentials to keep a person alive. Other refusals, however, may be legally binding.

If you decide to make an advance statement, we think it is essential that you consult your doctor first and then discuss the matter in detail with your family.

glossary

administrator/administratrix A person appointed by a probate registry or court to deal with the deceased's estate, where the deceased did not leave a will.

assets All the property belonging to a person; this includes house, other land, stocks, shares, money in a bank account or savings account, car, furniture, jewellery and so on.

attestation clause A statement at the end of a will which says that the will has been properly signed and witnessed.

beneficiary A person who benefits under a will.

bequeath A word meaning to leave property to someone in a will; old-fashioned wills have the words 'I bequeath to...'; modern wills are more likely to use the words 'I give...'.

bequest A gift of something other than cash left in a will; it can be a gift of things such as money or shares or items such as a car, jewellery, a painting, furniture, etc.

bona vacantia Goods (or a whole estate) for which no owner can be found; the term is used for an estate when there is no one to inherit it; in this case the goods go to the Crown.

caveat A notice entered at a probate registry to prevent the grant of probate being made without notice being given to the person who entered the caveat; a caveat will be entered where there is some doubt about the validity of the will or where there is a dispute about who is entitled to act as executor.

chattels Goods which are 'moveable', that is items such as furniture, cars, yachts, jewellery, clothing, etc.

confirmation of executor (Scot.) The procedure to appoint someone as an executor so that they can deal with the estate; special forms need to be filled in for this.

contingent gift A gift left in a will with a condition attached, for example that the beneficiary will only inherit when they reach the age of 21.

devise A gift of land; old-fashioned wills are likely to have the words 'I devise to … my house and land at …'; modern wills are more likely to use the words 'I give'.

executor/executrix A person named in a will or appointed by a court to deal with the deceased's estate, where the deceased left a will.

grant of probate The court's permission for an executor to collect in the deceased's assets, pay the debts and then distribute the estate to those named in the will.

holograph will (Scot.) A will made before 1 August 1995 which was completely hand-written by the testator; if the testator had signed such a will, it would be valid even though there were no witnesses.

inter vivos Literally 'between living persons'; a gift inter vivos is a gift made during the person's lifetime and is not what is left to him under a will.

intestacy Where a person has died without making a valid will.

intestate A person who dies without making a valid will.

legacy A gift left to someone in a will.

legal rights (Scot.) The rights of a widow(er) and children to part of the estate.

letters of administration The court's permission for an administrator to collect in the deceased's assets, pay the debts and then distribute the estate to those who inherit under the rules of intestacy.

prior rights (Scot.) The rights of a widow(er) to inherit the first part of the deceased's estate when there is no will.

probate Legal confirmation that a will is valid and that the executors have authority to deal with the estate.

residuary estate/residue The remainder of an estate after debts, funeral and other expenses and tax have been paid and all specific legacies distributed.

revoke To legally cancel a will.

specific legacy A gift in a will of a specific thing, e.g. a car or a painting, or a gift of a specific amount of money, e.g. a legacy of £5,000.

testator/testatrix Testator is the legal term for the person making a will; testatrix is the feminine form of the word so this means a woman who has made a will.

testing clause (Scot.) A statement at the end of a will which says that the will has been properly signed and witnessed.

trust A legal arrangement to hold money or other property for another person; a trust is usually set up when it provides tax advantages or where a beneficiary is a child.

trustee A person appointed to hold property on behalf of another under a trust.

checklist of assets

Home	£
Other property	£
Household contents	£
Valuables	£
Furniture/antiques	£
Jewellery	£
Car(s)	£
Boat	£
Savings and cash	£
Stocks and shares	£
Other investments	£
Pension benefits	£
Life assurance	£
TOTAL ASSETS	£

useful address

Probate Registries

The Principal Probate Registry

London
Principal Registry of the Family Division,
Probate Department,
First Avenue House,
42–49 High Holborn,
London, WC1V 6 NP
Tel: 020 7947 7000

There are also District Probate Registries at main centres around the country.

Birmingham
Birmingham District Probate Registry,
The Priory Courts,
33 Bull Street,
Birmingham,
B4 6DU
Tel: 0121 681 3400/3414

Brighton
Brighton District Probate Registry,
William Street,
Brighton,
BN2 2LG
Tel: 01273 684071

Bristol
Bristol District Probate Registry,
Ground Floor,
The Crescent Centre,
Temple Back,
Bristol,
BS1 6EP
Tel: 0117 927 3915 / 926 4619

Cardiff
Cardiff District Probate Registry,
Probate Registry of Wales,
2 Park Street,
Cardiff,
CF1 1TB
Tel: 029 2037 6479

Ipswich
Ipswich District Probate Registry,
Haven House,
17 Lower Brook Street,
Ipswich,
Suffolk,
IP4 1DN
Tel: 01473 231951

Leeds
Leeds District Probate Registry,
3rd Floor,
Coronet House,
Queen Street,
Leeds,
LS1 2BA
Tel: 0113 243 1505

Liverpool
Liverpool District Probate Registry,
The Queen Elizabeth II Law Courts,
Derby Square,
Liverpool,
L2 1XA
Tel: 0151 236 8264

Manchester
Manchester District Probate Registry,
9th Floor,
Astley House,
Quay Street,
Manchester,
M3 4AT
Tel: 0161 834 4319

Newcastle upon Tyne
Newcastle District Probate Registry,
2nd Floor,
Plummer House,
Croft Street,
Newcastle upon Tyne,
NE1 6NP
Tel: 0191 261 8383

Oxford
Oxford District Probate Registry,
Oxford Combined Court Building,
St Aldgates,
Oxford,
OX1 1LY
Tel: 01865 793 055

Winchester
Winchester District Probate Registry,
4th Floor,
Cromwell House,
Andover Road,
Winchester,
Hampshire,
SO23 7EW
Tel: 01962 863771

There are also several Sub Registries in England and Wales. These are in:

Bangor	Gloucester	Norwich
Bodmin	Lancaster	Nottingham
Carlisle	Leicester	Peterborough
Carmarthen	Lincoln	Sheffield
Chester	Maidstone	Stoke-on-Trent
Exeter	Middlesbrough	York

The telephone numbers of these Sub District Registries can be found in local telephone books. The addressess and telephone numbers of all the registries can be found on the web at www.lawontheweb.co.uk

Scotland

Sheriff Clerk (Commissary Office),
16 North Bank Street,
Edinburgh,
EH1 2NS

Sheriff Clerk of Glasgow and Strathkelvin,
County Buildings,
149 Ingram Street,
Glasgow,
G1 1SY

Northern Ireland

The Master, Probate and Matrimonial Office,
Royal Courts of Justice,
Chichester Street,
Belfast,
BT1 3JE

Capital Taxes offices

For all England and Wales, except Newcastle District Probate Registry

Ferrers House,
PO Box 38,
Castle Meadow Road,
Nottingham,
NG2 1BB
Tel: 0845 2341020
Fax: 0115 974 2432

Scottish applications and Newcastle District Probate Registry

Mulberry House,
16 Picardy Place,
Edinburgh,
EH1 3NB
Tel: 0131 556 8511
Fax: 0131 556 9894

Northern Ireland

Level 2,
Dorchester House,
52–58 Great Victoria Street,
Belfast,
BT2 7BB
Tel: 01232 315556
Fax: 01232 331001

Inland Revenue (For payment of IHT)

For all England and Wales, except Newcastle District Probate Registry

Financial Services Office (IHT Cashiers),
Inland Revenue (A),
Barrington Road, Worthing,
West Sussex,
BN12 4XH

For Scotland and Newcastle District Probate Registry

Central Accounting Office,
Head Office Scotland,
Mulberry House,
16 Picardy Place,
Edinburgh,
EH1 3NB

Other useful addresses

Charity Commissioners,
Harmsworth House,
13–15 Bouverie Street,
London,
EC4Y 8DP
Tel: 0870 330 0123
www.charity-commission.gov.uk

Court of Protection,
Stewart House,
24 Kingsway,
London,
WC2B 6JX
Tel: 020 7269 7000

The Official Solicitor and
Public Trustee,
Estates Acceptance Office,
81 Chancery Lane,
London, WC2A 1DD
Tel: 020 7911 7127
www.offsol.demon.co.uk

London Gazette,
PO Box 7923,
London,
SW8 5WF
Tel: 020 7873 8308
www.gazettes-online.co.uk

Counselling and support

The following are the head offices of the organizations. Addresses and telephone numbers of local support groups can be found in local telephone directories.

Age Concern England,
Astral House,
1268 London Road,
London,
SW16 4ER
Tel: 020 88765 7200
www.ageconcern.org.uk

National Associations of Widows,
National Office,
48 Queens Road,
Coventry,
CV1 3EH
Tel: 024 7663 4848
www.widows.uk/net

Age Concern Wales,
1 Cathedral Road
Cardiff,
CF11 9SD
Tel: 029 2037 1566
www.accymru.org.uk

CRUSE (bereavement care),
CRUSE House,
126 Sheen Road,
Richmond,
Surrey,
TW9 1UR
Tel: 020 8939 9530
www.crusebereavementcare.org.uk

Age Concern Northern Ireland,
3 Lower Crescent,
Belfast, BT7 1NR,
Tel: 028 9024 5729
www.ageconcern.org.uk

Age Concern Scotland,
113 Rose Street,
Edinburgh,
EH2 3DT
Tel: 0131 220 3345
www.ageconcernscotland.org.uk

Disclaimer

The publisher has used its best endeavours to ensure that the URLs for external websites referred to in this book are correct and active at the time of going to press. However, the publisher has no responsibility for the websites and can make no guarantee that a site will remain live or that the content is or will remain appropriate.

index